THE WORLD IS STUPID— YOU CAN'T FIX IT!

But Could Something Be Done?

Claude Roessiger

iUniverse, Inc.
Bloomington

The World is Stupid—You Can't Fix It!
But Could Something Be Done?

iUniverse books may be ordered through booksellers or by contacting:

iUniverse
1663 Liberty Drive
Bloomington, IN 47403
www.iuniverse.com
1-800-Authors (1-800-288-4677)

ISBN: 978-1-4502-7667-2 (pbk)
ISBN: 978-1-4502-7668-9 (cloth)
ISBN: 978-1-4502-7669-6 (ebk)

Library of Congress Control Number: 2010918102

Printed in the United States of America

iUniverse rev. date: 12/6/2010

Is life no more than a tale told by an idiot,
full of sound and fury, signifying nothing?

Not quite, but almost.

Introduction
The world is full of prostitutes.
An honest whore makes us a better friend.

My editor, and also close friends who are such because they are unfailingly honest with me, have criticized this manuscript on several broad points beyond the details that can always benefit from an independent reading. I have taken account of their criticisms of some of the points and made appropriate revisions. On other points I have chosen, upon reflection, not to make any changes but rather to confront the points in an introduction—an introduction I had not originally intended at all.

The modern habit in commentary is to develop a substantiated case, something akin to an academic thesis. This involves extensive citations and footnotes, ostensibly to prove the author's case. This was not always so. Marcus Aurelius composed his *Meditations* without footnotes, and Descartes eschewed them in *Les Discours de la Méthode* as well. The preamble to the Declaration of Independence affirms broad truths, without reliance on citations or expert opinions, and so does Tom Paine's *Common Sense.* I do not think that the current fashion for documentation serves any but a cosmetic purpose in a commentary— even a polemic if you will. It clouds the argument as much as it reveals it.

There is no art to picking and choosing one's citations. Any case can be substantiated with apparently expert opinions, and any case may be broken down by the same. The Internet is a ready source for expert opinions—pro, con, and just confused—upon pretty much any subject of inquiry. It serves no purpose to direct the modern reader to one set of sources when so many are so readily available. The criticism made to me—that I make rather sweeping declarations seemingly blithely—is fair if the reader wishes it so. But with full respect, the declarations I have made are to my best belief broadly correct, and this may in our day be easily verified with the help of Google and a few minutes of one's time. I can only hope that the arguments presented offer sufficient weight by common sense and common experience that a reader will delve further into any matter that he may question.

A second point that was mentioned to me—and the critique is a fair one—is that the narrative seems to hop around a bit. Probably it does, but no more than what was common in classical polemics which more followed the form of a conversation—a dialogue between friends perhaps—than a thesis. What I hope to have avoided is any sort of haphazard hopping around, which could only be sloppiness on my part.

The matter of giving the reader a suggestion of my purpose was raised. It is this: we have before us, it seems to me more so than in the past, but I acknowledge that this might miss the perspective of other times, a series of beliefs—palpably false—that have come to greatly influence public policy. Beyond the vast waste of finite resources that these policies impose is the destruction of liberty that they entail. I take liberty as an unalienable right, an irrefutable good. If I may by raising questions regarding these beliefs help to bring a more critical eye upon them, I shall have succeeded in my purpose. If this more critical eye will in some small way help to restore lost liberty, I shall be well rewarded.

Last is the matter of somehow crafting a polemic that is not a rant. No one much appreciates a rant, and inevitably we question the author's equanimity. Bitterness is a poor guide, but anger is not always so. There is justifiable anger; the American Revolution was surely that, in speech and in musket fire. There was nothing unsettled to be found in Washington's mind. The title that came to me for this book, avowedly provocative, is too negative, I've been told. Americans like optimistic themes. I do, too. Yet, the cure to this illness upon us can only be found by understanding it well and rooting it out. In the Western social democracies, we have too much favored fairy tales over reality; we don't like the sometimes uncomfortable reality. My philosophy has been that we should confront it.

C. R.

Chapter 1
A Tale Told by an Idiot

If we squint our eyes and peer back to an ancient plain beneath an ancient sun, if we imagine our ancestors thereupon, massed and brutish and fearful, if we see these inchoate men through the hot dust lifted by their tramping feet, it is difficult not to also see the one before them, leading them—their leader. And therein is the tale.

Who is this leader we seem so to need and far too often to revere? This hero of epics, this victor in war, this giver of law, this tyrant, this murderer? And what is the stuff of those who follow—the followers, the people, the mass, the dumb herd? Is this ancient story not a curious and painful tale?

If we are saved, if we are to be saved, if man is somehow more than a brutish beast of no account led by a handful of alpha creatures, we can find optimism only in a divine spark. Let us hope for it and pray for it. Without it, the denouement is too awful to contemplate. I speak practically, not religiously.

The inspiration—for such it was, sudden and complete—for this book arose in a single moment when thoughts accumulated over a lifetime coalesced. A window opened upon a broad field whereupon all of the elements stood ordered and interconnected. Do not mistake me: I refer not to a vision, or anything like it. No! Rather, a puzzle whose disjointed pieces have long been left on the table unassembled, and to which the solution is of a sudden seen. Call it a moment of insight, the eureka moment that is now increasingly understood as a very real phenomenon.

What were the pieces of this puzzle? Many. But at the core was always the existence of a masterpiece, a keystone, and that broadly speaking the essence of it was liberty and man, perhaps—not necessarily religiously—the soul of man. The question was and is "Can man be man without liberty?" We tilt toward philosophy with such a query, but we will not enter upon philosophy's province even if our pursuit leads to philosophical considerations. The questions we shall pose do not have easy, ready answers. We must think deeply. Do other pieces to the puzzle exist? Oh, sure. Can man be free? Does man want to be free? Does it matter?

We have learned that somehow the progression of Western thought led man from the dark cavern of the ancient world, where a man was no more than a beast of modest value, undifferentiated from the mass of men, to the modern world, where enlightenment made each man precious in his own right ... and a beast of modest value, undifferentiated from the mass of men. What changed? What did not?

We will leave the epistemological questions to the great thinkers; it was probably in the nature of things that their questions would lead to answers that are in fact only further queries, the unknown leading to the unknowable. Instead we will consider how the world may be stupid, and why we cannot fix it. This would seem a pessimistic thesis. In a way, it is. But it is more than that. To have any hope of curing a disease, one must first understand its nature. No matter how awful the ill, it must be examined, palpated, smelled, and—yes—sometimes contracted before we can hope to conquer it. It's a journey we shall take together.

We will begin with the nature of society's organization, which is after all in the nature of man. We have all learned at some time one of those platitudes that glide by us as we gaze numbly out of a classroom window, that man is a social animal. Well, he is, isn't he? With the exception of a few hermits—inevitably the butt of jokes that betray our suspicion of solitude—we gather in societies. It may be that we have some need for each other's company, to view the social animal through one lens, or it may be that we gather for protection, as a school of fish, to view it through another lens. Which is true? It matters, even if our common-sense experience suggests to us that it's some of both.

Various theories explain the origin of government. The political theorist Mancur Olson elaborated the theory of the "stationary bandit." It runs this way: Man as a solitary creature found himself vulnerable. He banded into groups. One among the group was brighter, swifter, stronger, better looking, or what have you, and became the group leader. Capable leaders were more successful than less capable ones, and groups led by capable leaders became tribes. At the time man was a hunter-gatherer, so the tribe that hunted and gathered more successfully became larger. Those who did a bad job were sent to extinction without passing Go. Those who managed to survive joined a more successful tribe. Success, then as now, was defined by the accretion of goods: food, shelter, utilitarian things, pretty things, women. This led to plunder. In fact, in Mancur Olson's words, the successful hunting group became "roving bandits." And they were ordinarily led by a stronger leader, a roving bandit himself. As the basic necessities became reasonably assured for the group, and as some sort of division of labor and good organization liberated some time for mischievous pursuits, the roving bandit's eye fell increasingly upon trinkets and nubile creatures, suggesting the need for a place to keep the newfound booty. Ah! A tent, a hut, a house, a manor, a castle, a walled town, and—presto—the roving bandit parked the horse and became a stationary bandit.

It doesn't take a bridge of much account to understand that the stationary bandit is what we call government. The instincts of government are those of a thief and a tyrant, and a man who wants to be free is left to defend himself against—let's be clear, historically this means to kill—the stationary bandit. Not so easy. The stationary bandit has an elaborate security apparatus designed to protect him against exactly this eventuality, but another fact remains: *his slaves prefer to be slaves.* Shocking? Let us continue, for herein is the essence of our inquiry: if the world is stupid and it cannot be fixed, it's because the component parts somehow aren't right. The component parts are human beings. An even cursory study of history supports this view, however antithetical it seems to us: man has spent most of his existence on this planet as a slave, a subject, a serf, a brutish beast led by a small number of strong leaders, sometimes led unwillingly but far more tragically and frequently led willingly. The times—indeed they are hardly even moments but only instants—of enlightenment and grace are few, so few that one can count them upon a single hand, whereas those of oppression and darkness require the gathered hands of us all to fairly count them ...and even then one will want for fingers. *Oppression and darkness are the natural state of man.*

In the Western world, we are or think of ourselves as, terrible evidence to the contrary aside, children of the Enlightenment. Well, not so fast. In what someone called the terrible twentieth century, more men killed other men than in any other century in history. Enlightenment? There was a distinction between us and previous incarnations of humanity, it's true: some of us were horrified. In classical times no one gave mass slaughter any particular thought; our ancient brethren were more realistic than we and considered it the way of the world, the spoil of the victor, the right of the stronger, or somehow, intuitively, the survival of the fittest. Maybe it was. Some historians have advanced the argument that more advanced societies annihilate less advanced ones, barely leaving unspoken the implication that it's not a bad thing. Be the implication as it may, the axiom stands: more advanced societies triumph over less advanced ones, whether it be suddenly with flashing swords and lopped-off heads, or over the longer course, by their comfort and ease unconsciously killing off the hungry and the poor, as in Africa today. It is not just by the sword of the strong that men die, but also by the hand of disdainful good intentions. The comfort and ease of the wealthy suggests in the current time—with self-satisfaction put first, as always—that it would be a good thing if the poor were not so poor ... so just mandate it.

This in one guise is called "fair trade," whereby we ensure the increased prosperity of the already not-so-poor and guarantee the death—literally, not figuratively—of the world's poorest. Under the Fair Trade Doctrine, we will only buy goods produced by those who receive some guaranteed "fair price" for their labor. Unfortunately—a small failing of economic understanding—one cannot mandate a fair price in the place of a market price, and when one does one *always* either creates a black market or some kind of monopoly. And, damn the downtrodden! We shall revert to this topic. It is only one among many examples.

We fast forward now, from ancient man through classical man to modern man and the revolutionary movement that hit its stride with the French Revolution. What a marvel that was: the template for the horrors of communism a century in advance! It is true that the French Revolution had some threads similar to those of the American Revolution—which was far more a social revolution than a war of secession, in spite of what England thought—but it's also true that in spite of both having had a common ground in the Enlightenment, they took divergent paths. Whether their ultimate destinations will be very different remains to be seen; they are surely less different than once thought. France today has an oppressive government. So has the United States. The glory of the stationary bandit! From the smoke and the blood of the French Revolution came a Marxist revolutionary fervor that is with us yet, the slain Soviet and Maoist hosts having expired without taking with them the disease that killed them. We shall inquire into the nature of this disease, for it is one that greatly afflicts us. Stupidity? Yes, in fact. How can one try an experiment in every conceivable way for over a century, without ever finding the least suggestion of success, killing hundreds of millions of men and women in the process, and continue to try? It's as silly as the old alchemist's dream of turning lead into gold. It's very wrong! In fact, it's much more than that: it's savagely and criminally stupid. But this is the nature of man, and it makes our world.

As we do not seem able to free ourselves from the virus of socialism in all its Hydra-like guises, we will do well to understand its nature. In the modern language of technology, this virus enters the body as a

Trojan horse, masquerading as good. Upon having successfully invaded the body, it turns upon its host and shows itself for what it is and ever has been: a stationary bandit, a tyrant, and a murderer, one more sad chapter in man's inhumanity to man.

The lyrics to its siren song are sweet: "a human face," "life in harmony with nature," "equality"— the *égalité* that continues to plague the French—"human rights," "peace," and all the nostrums of youthful idealism. Its reality is much harsher: the dictatorship of the proletariat that turns out to be just another dictatorship; violence and repression; equality divided—equality of privilege for the masters and equality of misery for the serfs; the wholesale destruction of nature[1] in the construction of the New World Order—that self-serving bromide about not making an omelet without breaking a few eggs; and the grinding into ashes of the human spirit.

In fact, however it's cooked or tossed, socialism ends up being about power, the strong over the weak, wreaking upon the world the terrible dreams of their own fevers. Socialism sweetens its bitter medicine with the sugar of newspeak, wherein words are given meanings exactly opposite to their plainly understood ones. It was not a trivial notion when the prophet Isaiah enjoined "not to take bitter for sweet, dark for light, or evil for good." The misuse of language, a reflection of the decline of critical thought, assured by the relativism and dumbing-down of education, is a root cause and component of oppression. Penny-ante tyrants fashion themselves kings. The people gawp and take the bait. Without a rigorous education, liberty fails.

But we have digressed from our thesis while explaining it: at the heart of our misery is ...ourselves. We cannot posit a stupid world without coming to understand that it is man who makes it so—primitive, atavistic, tribal, fearful, superstitious man. We see in the mirror all the brush strokes of modernity, but we don't see that the paint never dried,

---

1   It is not by accident that the most awful pollution and despoliation of nature occurred and occurs in authoritarian states; there is no effective contrary opinion. Socialist states, governments wherein the state controls a half, more or less, of the economy, are inherently authoritarian, as they cannot exist without being so, which will be discussed in more depth later.

and that it takes only a few scrapes of the knife to reveal the primitive being, dull-browed and unenlightened, cowering before thunder, scurrying in the night lest magical forces ensnare him, whispering the most fantastic tales to his credulous and fey fellows.

There is security in the tribe: anything is better than standing alone. Liberty means standing alone, with the free man rendered sufficient unto himself by his enlightenment. Better to compromise liberty for security. If the price to pay for security is serfdom, so be it. The night is too frightful. *And thus does man choose slavery.* We saw recently how easily Americans, shocked and frightened beyond reason by the events of 9/11, gave up their fundamental liberties to gain what they thought might be some increase of security. Alas it wasn't to be, and never was. As Franklin observed, those who think to give up liberty for security lose both. Americans of the revolutionary generation, or even of the nineteenth century, themselves within some sort of living memory of the Revolution, would never have reacted thus to 9/11; they would have understood that safety lies in courage.

The question is—now, later, in the futures of our children's children—whether there is any hope. The answer is "Maybe, some." It is not a sure thing. History can only make us doubt. The glory of Beethoven's Symphony no. 9 restores our faith. So we continue.

The slave of ancient Egypt, the serf of the medieval manor, and the citizen of our modern social democracies have this much in common: some kind of security in the place of liberty. All are bound by force. You think not? Try not to pay your taxes in one of our modern social democracies. Then, return to this paragraph, chastened. What is a tax but a seizing of man's labor, a medium of exchange by which the labor is given to the prince in fungible rather than literal form? Oh sure, there is a difference. I'm being deliberately provocative. The hypothesis in our modern states is that "we tax ourselves." That is since long years a canard. We only imagine to do so. In fact what happens is that the stationary bandit buys the votes by which to do what he wants, so there is an appearance of common cause with the people, but this is a chimera: a bought vote is a corrupt vote, and it means nothing. It is in its own way a coerced vote, as empty as the votes used to elect the Politburo in the Soviet State.

Indeed, in the second chapter, we shall explore the essential corruption of modern social democracy. The economic rule is rather simple: when taxes begin to pay for wants rather than needs, the fabric of corruption is woven as factions vie for influence and money. In our social democracies, the wants today are preponderant, the needs often neglected. The wants are no more than latter-day Roman circuses. This is why we have billions for the teachers union's pet projects—of no value to education but assuring their votes—and kids who can't read, while our roads fall apart.

One thing however is historically clear: socialism doesn't work, collectivism is a dud, and authoritarian states inevitably fall to freer states, until they themselves become authoritarian—the sad and apparently unavoidable fruit of success. This thesis was the subject of a recent inquiry whereby a historian examined key battles, the turning points in the course of Western civilization: Alexander's annihilation of a Persian army five times greater than his own, for example, and Lepanto another. The conclusion was that collectivist armies and societies, rigid by their natures, fall to freer and more flexible ones. Thus, the great advances occur remarkably swiftly—instants in time—when flexible, freer societies have their moment in the sun, as during the first three centuries of the Ottoman Empire, at the time the most liberal and arguably benign society on the planet. China may be living such a moment in the sun right now, with the rapid dismantling of the collectivist hell under which it suffered and starved—Mao's socialist paradise—and the manumission of the clever and creative Chinese to do their own thing. The result is indisputable: three decades of the most remarkable growth in prosperity ever seen in the history of man … and no one starving anymore. This will no more be forever than it ever was for any people, but it may give the Chinese a good twenty-first century. They are in that sweet spot where the revenues of the state are not yet punitive upon the people, and thus they are able to be sufficient unto themselves.

It is one of the great jokes—ironies—of our time that a state that pretends to be communist is in fact one of the freest and fastest growing markets on the planet. So much for communism. The ruling junta have been clever: they just changed the meaning of the word. Their success is for the moment underpinned by the extraordinary growth of the tribe's wealth. Indeed, it is thought a delicate balance, and there is palpable concern that should that growth fail the junta might be at risk. So for the moment growth it is, to the enormous benefit of the tribe. But let that growth bring broad prosperity, as it will, and we can be sure of one thing: the people will exchange the freedom—and risk—that brought them that prosperity for greater security, with the result that they will give up their newfound freedom, and the junta will seek to ensure its continued survival with the distribution of the snake oil of social democracy.

If we blame the junta, we blame the wrong thing. It is man himself who is to blame. The question can be whether it is in fact somehow rational—it may be—to choose to go for broke when one has nothing, there being nothing to lose, but to choose security when one has something, wishing to safeguard it. However there is the conundrum: the path of security is the path of ultimate decline. True security—success—lies in the willingness to accept risk, to accept Admiral Lord Nelson's dictum that "The bold course is the safe course." Right at war, right at peace. The meek may one day inherit the earth, but not for now.

I do not make a devil of socialism. It is an economic notion, wrongheaded by experience, born in people of mostly good impulses, and often used by demagogues in the pursuit of power. It's an easy sale; it sounds so benign. We ought not to be surprised. After all, physicians bled patients, at times literally to death, seeking their cure. No one seemed to notice that no cure ever came. What can one say? I avoid, however, the demonization of socialism; it speaks for itself. Mine is not a knee-jerk criticism. It is a reasoned and reflected one based upon incontestable evidence. We spoke earlier of socialism's Hydra-headed guises. Let us examine that further.

Socialism is a collective organization of society, whereby somehow the labor of the individual belongs to the collective for the common good. Thus slavery, which after all was the condition of most men for most of man's history, is a form of socialism. So was serfdom, a modified form of slavery wherein the fetters were broken, but the principle retained. In the Hitlerian, Marxist-Leninist, and Maoist constructs the "liberation" of the working class was—tricky of them, but it sold—in fact the enslavement of the working class and pretty much everyone else, under the pretense of a future greater good. This resembled the Medieval Church, which traded obedience for salvation, another form of subjugation and tribute. After the truly unbelievable horrors wrought upon man by the socialist-communist-totalitarian regimes of the twentieth century, at least communism got a bad name, and socialism, its theoretical bedmate, a bad odor. So for a time these became unsalable. This led to a repackaging of the old product under the new banner of environmentalism, regarding which we'll have something to say in a later chapter. But let us make no error: environmentalism has as little to do with conservation, its honest antecedent, as—in Mark Twain's words—lightning has to do with a lightning bug.

What strikes us in viewing the world with perspective, what the French call *recul*, is how some among us, in each generation, not only think they know better than their fellows but want to impose their vision upon others. These are the alpha males and females described by social science. A tendentious argument could be made that there ought to be mandatory genetic testing of newborns, and those who test positive for the alpha gene ought to be exposed as undesirable babes, as in Roman times, and done away with. The argument would be a good one if we could separate the alphas destined for tyranny from those destined for vaulting works of glory, the paradox being that it is alphas who destroy us and alphas who elevate us. This paradox is not so shocking; even our own minds sometimes lead us and sometimes mislead us. How to sort one alpha from the other?

There is no present and moral way to isolate the bad alphas. We know that we are on a path, as uncomfortable as we sense it may be,

A Tale Told by an Idiot

to genetic testing for potentially too many things. Without inclining toward Luddite views, some areas of scientific progress will need to be considered in the future for their bearing on what we have taken as our basic rights. Perhaps the right to privacy, as awkward as its application was when applied to the matter of abortion, will have to be more concretely added to our constitutional rights.

But I digress: back to the bad alphas. The only approach we have seen that at least constrains the worst instincts of these rogues is constitutional, limited government, with "constitutional" and "limited" being separate qualities. The emphasis is required because large government, albeit constitutional, is a playground for bad alphas. They just take the thing over. Therefore, constitutional and limited. And, were that the entire solution, it might work. But bad alphas have many tricks. They have long years since learned to co-opt constitutions, to twist them and mangle them and bend them, so that the original plain language, which any ten people drawn from the telephone directory would similarly understand, comes to mean things that cannot be found in the words at all. Or, by applying newspeak as the Soviets did, an ostensibly noble constitution is made over into a bludgeon of oppression. Most of us have some atavistic understanding of treason, and that treason is a bad and serious matter, so a law against it seems reasonable enough. But for an alpha, only a very small step exists between the betrayal of the nation and the betrayal of his person and will—the alpha leader usually joins his person to the nation—such that a traitor becomes much easier to define: anyone who disagrees with him. Therein lies the mischief.

Mischief is by its nature cascading. Let a leader be a tyrant, and he will breed an entire flock of small tyrants beneath him, arrayed in the most jealous of pecking orders. Thus does tyranny become complete: the people afraid, broken, and harnessed. On the face of it we disdain tyranny, but things aren't that simple. Remember how the world really is. In any population, we can always find those who imagine that in some way they can benefit from the tyranny: the leader, the leadership, their pals, minor alphas, lackeys, thugs, and layabouts. To use a round number, for the sake of argument, call these a fifth or so of the population.

Then there are the little people—I do not say it with disdain but with enormous respect—who for very understandable reasons hope only to somehow survive, to go from day to day in some kind of peace, to raise their children with some sort of decency. How many? Well, say two-fifths in a modern society, again for sake of argument. In the Third World the little people can be four-fifths of the population, 80 percent. They are mostly passive and easy to cow.

The remainder are troublesome for the tyrant, say up to 40 percent in a modern social democratic society, and a much smaller number—"dangerous revolutionaries"—in the Third World. Two solutions exist really: bribe them or terrorize them. Historically it can go either way. The bribes are of course paid with the money of the bribed. This is the misuse of taxation for what is sold as redistribution of income—a theory that passes for well intended until we realize that it isn't Robin Hood at all, but simply the dispensing of favors for votes, the already well-off often getting the disproportionate benefit. In this consideration we return to the distinction between the raising of revenue for the common need—the justifiable purpose of taxation—and the seizing of money by government force for the wants of factions, the first want of the governing faction being to remain in power. Were this once understood by the people, they would understand the power of their purse, and they would be much the stingier with their money. However, as a prescient nineteenth-century British prime minister foretold, the death of democracy is the realization by the people that they can help themselves to their own purse.

We live this now, where factions vie with each other to mount ever more grand circuses, of little or no purpose save the corruption of votes. This is generally called pork, and if it were confined to that which is commonly identified as pork, the problem would be but small; the tragic reality is that in the modern social democracies, pork constitutes well over half of the total budget. The consequences are terrible. Nations are ruined. Inflation—the great hidden tax—becomes the only palatable solution. The people are grown so accustomed to lard that no diet seems possible.

The alternative to pork is terror. For this, or at least its modern form, we have a French nobleman to thank: Robespierre, the classical rich kid in search of a cause who has inflicted so much suffering upon the world since the beginnings of time. The only justice in the thing was that this rich kid was soon enough himself presented to his favorite toy, the guillotine.

But I digress. Robespierre created the modern model for terror, the insight that "the purpose of terror is to terrify." With this understanding in hand, one can make terror vastly more efficient than under the constraint of having to actually find enemies to attack. One can attack anyone at random: Tuesday nights, those living in odd-numbered houses; Thursday nights, those with white pocket handkerchiefs (or, as the Inquisition did—also leading lights in the terror business— burning at the stake for heresy women who changed their underwear on a Saturday); and Sundays, those who go—or don't go—to holy services. It really doesn't matter. The purpose of terror is to terrify. The more random it is, the more it terrifies. If cows in a pasture come to understand that all white cows are kept for milk, but the black cows are led to the abattoir, the white cows will soon enough be tranquil; the trick is to keep them guessing.

That is the nature of effective terror: it leaves none unfrightened. No one.

In our modern social democracies, we pretend to have forsworn terror and chosen bribery—and to some extent that is true, of course. We avoid the long screams of the basement corridors of the Lubyanka, even if we have allowed ourselves Guantanamo.[2] But we operate terror

---

2   Some Americans forgave, or understood, or even supported Guantanamo on the justification of necessity in the face of terror. This is to sell one's soul to the devil. We are or we are not defenders of liberty and rights. Once we pick and choose who shall have rights, we fatally wound those rights, and it is only a matter of time until we shall lose our own rights. Martin Luther King Jr. explained this perfectly when he declared, "If I'm not free, you're not free." Rights cannot be half-rights. Rights cannot be for one but not for the other.

at a more subtle level. Ask those who have stood accused—without grounds—by the American, French, Italian, or German tax authorities. Ask them what it did to their lives. Ask them what compensation they received once, and if, the false accusation was ultimately dropped. As Aleksandr Solzhenitsyn commented about the Soviet Gulag, it was effective because deep down we have the feeling that if people are in prison, they must have done something ... after all, innocent people aren't put in prison. But they are.

So there we have it: bribery or terror. Ready to order?

Whether we can once understand the inefficiency and the inhumanity of the collective is improbable. We have not understood it in ten thousand years. It is difficult to imagine that it would suddenly dawn upon us. *Slavery—the collective—is the natural state of man.* Sorry, but that is what history tells us. Not nice. Just true.

Americans of the nineteenth and twentieth centuries grew up with the "Spirit of '76" and to some extent managed to keep the revolutionary flame of liberty burning over a remarkably long period—nearly two hundred years. This was the legacy granted the nation by surely one of the most remarkable confluences of history, that astonishing assembly of learned and wise men who found themselves together at the birth of the nation. To reread the preamble to the Declaration of Independence is to yet today bring tears to one's eyes, so powerful is the appeal to self-evident truths, liberty's voice. The very cadence of the words calls us with an immortal appeal.

No American politician writing today could give us the thought or the language of Jefferson. Here is what we miss in our contemporary understanding of the Spirit of '76: that it was only possible at a moment in time that brought together the thought of the Enlightenment and of

---

They are or they are not. Let once the wall be breached between the two, and we will find that it soon thereafter crumbles entirely. It is not accidental that concomitantly with Guantanamo, the constitutional rights of American citizens came to be routinely violated by their own government. The two pieces were of one whole. There is no such thing as being only a little bit pregnant; you are or you are not. The devil is a tough customer. Once he has a soul in hand, he isn't inclined to give it back.

the Scottish philosophers who spoke for it. Thus almost by accident in the American colonies, there came together a natural aristocracy of men of refined mind joined to a very small number of free yeomen, three million all told, spread over a vast and uninhabited land. The colonials themselves were not ordinary men and women—not at all!—but a handful taken from a much larger European population, a handful already inclined—by their immigration from the Old World, by their sense of adventure, by their pioneering spirit, by their determination, and by their beliefs—to liberty. These were rugged individuals, unafraid and strong.

Through a continuing immigration during the nineteenth century and into the early twentieth century, America refreshed herself generation by generation with an ever new stock of courageous men and women who mostly had left only misery behind for a new world of hope. They may have come off the boat ragged wretches, but by God they had the hearts of lions—not a milquetoast or a nervous Nellie among them! No safety warnings needed. No backing down. No turning back. Bridges burned. Eyes set on a far shore. Go find that in your suburban shopping mall, in your public school, at your club, in your company, and within your circle of friends. Hah! But *that* is why America was born a free nation, courage and enlightenment in equal measure in the crucible of its birth, its elemental steel tempered by the finest intellectual fire and annealed by the pure cold waters of reason. It's all gone now—long gone. Cowardly bullying stands in courage's place, and anodyne platitudes have replaced critical thought. Which of our wretches in Congress could discuss the great philosophers? Which could sort out Plato, Marcus Aurelius, Locke, and Mill? Empty noise reigns supreme. The poltroons have one purpose only: their re-elections, in the pursuit of which there is no posterior they will forbear kissing. Disgusting creatures.

When we come to understand the Spirit of '76—whence it came, whither it went—we also understand that the same sort of spirit animated those other rare instances of freedom that passed like shooting stars across the firmament of history. Fragile is freedom, unstable and delicate, a wisp no sooner perceived than gone. It is impossible to claim otherwise. All of history is against it. Stand upon a mount and look well up and down the grand river of time. Where do you see liberty?

Citizens of the modern social democracies were polled (in the 1990s) for their priorities. Only the Americans, the British and the Swiss put liberty high. The French chose equality—*l'égalité*; the Japanese elected social harmony; the Germans favored societal order; the Swedes opted for security. Now, just three-quarters of a generation later, who would still keep liberty high? We know what the Americans did: a small incident—historically speaking—on their soil in September of 2001 terrified them, and they ran to pawn their liberty for some sort—any sort—of security. A bad bargain. As Franklin had sagely predicted, they lost the one and didn't get the other.

Do not be fooled. Liberty is not natural to man. Slavery is. But before despair, we ought to choose inquiry—inquiry into the nature of the things of our times. We must try to understand where we have gone wrong and how we might yet go right. Perhaps liberty will surprise us yet, resurgent in the most unexpected of places—communist China, for instance, or socialist India. Liberty is the parent of prosperity. Prosperity has an undeniable appeal for the poor; let them once taste it and they will clamor for more. The spark is liberty. Perhaps China and India will then keep the flame for a time. It wouldn't be a bad thing, to see liberty experienced by half of humanity. That has never happened before.

Before we are done, we shall have examined the major issues of the day, the ones that constrain us and keep us from the next great advance—from a twenty-first-century enlightenment, from the prosperity that alone can meet the challenges of our futures.

There are animals that, led from a burning barn, will in their fear run back to their fiery stalls—imagining them secure—only to die. Let us not be they.

Chapter 2
Snake Oil: Social Democracy

The modern social democracies—we must be honest—are not so bad. It would be disingenuous to pretend otherwise. Their citizens do not know the misery that is ever a caller at the door of most of our planet's inhabitants; food is on the table; shelter is a given; care is available in infirmity; some kind of justice, relatively speaking, is offered; the wines are good and the cheeses varied. If we take the analogy of seeing the glass half full or half empty, we must confess that it is half full. But why only half full? That is the question.

If our premise is that we live in an enlightened age—a far more tendentious claim now than in the mid-nineteenth century—then, against a backdrop of stupefying scientific advances, we ought to be advancing what we could broadly call the manumission of man. But we are not. And as in empires past, our downfall is what it has ever been: corruption. The modern social democracies are now fundamentally and pervasively corrupt. Let us prove it to ourselves.

The underlying premise of our democracies is Lincolnian: government of, for, and by the people. For that to be, the people must be able to express themselves, to choose their leaders, to confirm those laws under which they will live, to tax themselves for common needs, and to keep for themselves all rights not ceded to the governing authority. In our social democracies, this understanding is now no more than hypothetical. What occurs in practice is that our governments have grown so large that a third of the people depend directly upon government for their livelihoods, and another third do so indirectly, in myriad ways. What is left is anything from a handful to perhaps—in the best of cases—a final third of the population that can be considered truly free of influence, the free citizens of classical philosophy. Curiously, our laws proscribe the buying of votes, calling for the severe punishment of the transgression, and yet we have suffered the buying of votes to have become institutionalized, with factions in government contesting the spoils of unrestrained taxation. We are complicit by the misunderstanding of an immutable economic law: we think we can tax our neighbor without having ourselves to pay.

In the nineteenth century, the French economist Frédéric Bastiat already described the reality: it is an illusion to suppose that a tax can be levied upon one member of a society without touching another. The notion of modern politics—that we can tax the rich, or smokers, or polluters, or whomever may be the target of the day—is a massive fraud. It cannot be done. A tax upon any member of a society is as a spoonful of water taken from a bowl; the entire water level will fall. To the extent that taxes are levied to pay for needs, that is as it should be, and all pay for what all will use. But as we have already seen, expenditures in our social democracies are now in their major part—and increasingly so as money is spent as by drunks on a binge—for wants.

By way of example, let us look at our schools, which account for a vast expenditure and an important component of our taxation. It is a well understood given that the high-school graduate of 1920 was much the better educated as against the one of today. At age eighteen or nineteen he received a diploma, a respected achievement that gave him a start in life. What is a high-school diploma today? Indeed, the once esteemed but now much degraded bachelor's degree has slipped into its former place. It is not so off the mark to think that even it may be inferior, in too many cases, to the high-school diploma of a century ago. Yet in real terms, we spend orders of magnitude more upon our schools than we did in 1920. Could we not have supposed that the extra money would secure a *better* result? Instead, it is worse—much worse. Ah, but where did the extra money go?

Our school of the 1920s was a rather basic thing: a roof, some heat in winter, some desks, respectable and respectably educated teachers who had actually acquired a diploma in the discipline they would teach, and a director. There might have been some sort of common sports field, maybe a simple and multipurpose gym—which surely doubled as the school's assembly hall—and not much else. Today such a school would be considered inadequate. It would be condemned, its door barred with a banner proclaiming it dangerous and substandard. Substandard how? Judged by needs or by wants? The need for a school is surely in the education it is able to give. On that count, our 1920s school wins hands down. Where does it come short? For the wants the educational establishment has hornswoggled us into taking for needs: galleys of administrators—in some schools, more than there are teachers; sports complexes that would do a professional team proud; guidance counselors who neither counsel nor guide; palatial buildings; every manner of equipment; swimming pools; auditoria; teaching assistants; disproportionately expensive facilities for the handicapped, whose education cannot be usefully conducted side-by-side with that of the other students anyway; budgets for every outlandish whim and social caprice; but—at the end of the day—a not very good record of literacy or numeration, without speaking of geography or history. The add-ons are always sold by appealing to expert opinion and to our better instincts. Which parents do not wish the best for their children? They are swindled as immigrant Irish widows used to be swindled by the undertakers, sold in their grief burials they could not afford, that Paddy might pass in as fine a style as Mick.

If our children cannot read properly, cannot count, do not know the difference between Austria and Australia, do not understand what an element is and think the periodic table something to be wary of for sex, are baffled about the causes of the American and French revolutions, are unable to comprehend a solipsism or a sophistry, cannot speak acceptably before a class, and think a foreign language is a Boston accent, we must judge our schools failures. They do not meet the *need*, never mind how splendidly outfitted they are for wants. The public-education establishment is one of the most powerful special interest groups in the nation, a union whose only purpose is its own perpetuation and aggrandizement. Who can still swallow their blather about excellence in education? We all know it's a joke—a rather sad one to be sure, made at the terrible expense of the next generation. Even the bright kids today are poorly educated, uncultured, and unrefined little boors whose brightness is discerned from the clever manipulation of a tablet containing printed circuits. By any measure, public education is an enormous gold brick for which we pay an extraordinary price, with a pittance for a result. What happened? We ceded our citizens' place as its overseers to self-appointed experts, individuals of no account and artful gamesters who redefined education to suit their own poor intellects. In many of our schools, the children might as well be guinea pigs in a laboratory run by a mad scientist; experimental notions are the rule, and when the kids turn out to be louts, well, we just go on to the next experiment. This is wicked. We know perfectly well how to educate children, and if the application of tried and true methods seems somehow to want for entertainment, so be it: at least as adults, they will have the opportunity for satisfying, productive lives. Our purpose in speaking of public education herein is not to reform it—that's a whole other subject—but to take it as an example of our system having gone off the rails, with enormous sums spent featherbedding and advancing a union, a very rich, powerful, and monopolistic union, giving up ever more of our capital—that is our labor—to pay for the whims and caprices of their failed establishment. Failed? Yes! However we measure the results, they give proof of a long decline. Yet, when it comes time to vote, they unfailingly get the money. Tom Wolfe spoke years ago about people being mau-maued in the pursuit of demands put up by vociferous interest groups. The people have been mau-maued by the educational establishment for many decades. What restaurant would keep its trade serving bad and expensive food night after night? So, why do we persist with this public education establishment?

Because they are a large group;

- Because public employees—of which the numbers are legion—support other public employees, an exercise in reciprocal back-scratching;
- Because the propaganda is good: "Don't you want the best for your child?" ("Yes, but you're not it," is the correct answer.)
- Because we have, through our own inferior and uncritical educations, ceded our rightful place of responsibility to "experts," on the premise that they must know better. (They don't in fact, being "expert" only by the acquisition of largely inferior academic degrees awarded by largely inferior academic programs, a grab bag of so-called education degrees.)
- Because the laws protecting the establishment have erected a protective wall around it, and attacks are repelled with burning oil. (Once you attain a certain level of power, you can have laws passed for you that protect you and advance your interests, a method that can only be called corrupt.)
- Because our rotten politicians count on the votes the educational establishment delivers, thus assuring their monopoly over education. (Do we think that the opposition to public funding of alternate private educational institutions is based on educational considerations? Let us not be naive. It is based on a monopoly that fights ferociously to maintain its monopoly power ... and the children be damned.)

The educational establishment is but one example of the corruption of social democracy. There are innumerable others. In many of our states is a law that requires the presence of a police officer at the site of road works, the officer in question being usually found dozing in his car, standing around scratching himself while yakking with an idle laborer, or gazing vacantly upon the passing traffic with the approximate light in his eyes of a cow in a pasture. Why? Because the police union mau-maued the legislature to enact this requirement, paid at overtime rates while using our equipment, to provide extra income for themselves. Value? Zero. Traditionally—remember when?—a construction worker with a flag would serve the purpose very well. Oh, yes: our police car is always running, using our gas, polluting our environment, and depreciating our equipment. The rationale? Well, you just never know when a fellow might be called to an emergency. He can't turn on the ignition quickly? The fire department does. Everywhere we look, we find this corruption. Everything that is touched by public money and is subject to a want rather than a need becomes a target for swindle.

Public highway departments are nests of sloth and inefficiency, with overlarge crews and equipment idle much of the time.

Health care—whithersoever it may go—now accounts in the United States for 16–17 percent of our GDP, a vast mismanaged engine of misapplied public money, regulation, and fat private interest gorging itself on idiotic public policy. Anyone old enough to remember house calls and a physician with time enough to recollect a patient's name can only shake his head in despair while, after a two-hour wait in an emergency room, having his temperature and blood pressure checked for a very visibly cut finger. But, by God, we'll have the best! So small-town dispensaries, now grandly called hospitals, make a public cause of installing multimillion-dollar MRI equipment, never mind that a hospital thirty minutes away has it already and that the local facility gets an itinerant technician who can actually operate the damned thing once every other Tuesday.

There is a simple rule, an economic verity as powerful as that of gravity in physics: do not mix public and private funds. It is and has ever been a formula for fiscal depravity. How many matching grants, inducements, and encouragements confront us? We cannot count them for their number. Do we remember how towns across the nation used the panic antiterrorism funds subsequent to the 9/11 incident? New buildings, swimming pools, every kind of toy our police and fire departments could lust for from their Big Toy Catalogue. My small town, which is about as likely a terrorist target as Ugly Betty is a one-night stand for Mick Jagger, bought itself a "four-wheeler"—get this—in case they needed to "retrieve bodies from the forest." Nobody guffawed, so inured are we to this sort of mindless nonsense. I think they also bought some diving equipment. You just never know when a terrorist submarine will turn up in a lake.

Speaking of the police, why are they always where we don't want them and never at hand when we do? It isn't by accident. Much of the country has far too many police. They sell "safety"—and who is against that?—but end up doing mischief: arresting and handcuffing teenagers with cigarettes or collecting taxes on roads with deliberately incorrectly posted speed limits, but when our homes are broken into, we are told to call the insurance company. We tolerate this because the police and fire services have become a massive lobby, because opposing them is on a par with shooting Bambi, because we have lost the courage that was once our birthright and now have the rigor and equanimity of a soccer mom, and because they get all their pals in public employ to beat the drums for them. Yet across much of America, we now have numbers in these functions—I do not even enter upon the subject of temperaments—which have no justification in public need.

If we speak of the military, which most of us do consider a need, who does not doubt the extraordinary waste to which it is subject? This is not innocent waste—waste by error, so to speak. It is deliberate and wanton waste, the stripping of the taxpayer for the purchase of votes. It is so scandalous that we now buy weapons systems that the brass themselves declare useless! Why? Because a congressman in one state wants it for jobs back home (votes) and all the other thieves in the gang (Congress) obediently vote for his laser-guided blowgun, so that when their own turbo-copter is up for a vote, the favor will be reciprocated (honor among thieves). Thus do the incumbents remain eternally in office, and thus are we complicit, seduced by the lucre they dispense. In the 2008–2009 emergency spending measure requested by the executive branch and approved by the legislature, over eight hundred spending items were added that were of no utility to us and that were not a part of the economic recovery package at all, to ensure the legislative votes of representatives who above all were interested—in a time of national crisis—in simply continuing to buy the votes back home to ensure their re-elections. It's unconscionable. We are as guilty as they are. But you see, our votes have been bought. We are just delivering on the bribe we have received. Everywhere we look, when we find that public moneys are expended for wants in the place of needs, we find corruption. Everywhere that we find public and private funds mixed, we find corruption. In the end our democracy exists only in name. We vote, but our votes are in large part as much in doubt as the votes Joe Stalin received in Soviet elections. I will grant, however, that should we err and vote incorrectly, there is this nuance: in a social democracy we are not normally shot for it. There is *nothing*, however, to be done for it. Our politicians thundering about transparency and accountability has become as laughable as it is in sub-Saharan Africa. There is far too much public money for any conceivable need. We have made needs of wants. The corruption is inherent, ineluctable, and intransigent. There is no chance—meaning zero—that our engorged and parasitic legislatures would ever reform the system. Has the Mafia ever given up crime?

The obdurate difficulty is that we have become addicts within this system, utterly deprived of the free will that constitutes a free citizen. Either we take the monies because they are set before us—Margaret Thatcher's irrefutable dictum that if one places hundred-pound notes along the motorway, motorists will stop to collect them—or because we are made cynical: why ought I to be the only chump who doesn't take the money? If I don't, the other guy will. I might as well. In my small town, we have bought many things we didn't need on this basis, including a very expensive fire engine so large that it cannot get around the village—it's too long to make the turns—but equipped with a fine ladder capable of reaching about twice the height of any building in town. How were we sold this white elephant? "If we don't take it"—the matching grant, in this case—"it'll just go elsewhere." Thus we not only wasted other taxpayers' hard-earned money, but we were also corrupted into wasting more of our own. Whose opinion did we take? Ah, yes, our fire chief's—our "expert." Apparently he doesn't have a tape measure.

Moreover, this corruption of money has led to a corruption of rights. Our Constitution is specific that those rights not enumerated and granted to the federal government are reserved for the states or for the people themselves. Those who have actually read the dialogues and debates around the adoption of the Constitution will know that this reservation of rights—or the prohibition of the federal government arrogating them to itself—was the subject of great concern among the founders. They were correct in their concern. The federal power, doing what power always does and seeking its own aggrandizement, came to see—as a result of the disproportionate and vast revenue growth it tested as a result of three vast wars (Civil War, WWI, WWII)—that it could withhold funds from the states in order to impose its will upon them.

Thus were the states told, for example, in the instance of the ridiculous national speed limit of the 1970s and 1980s, that if they did not enact the limit, they would lose federal highway funds. This has a name: blackmail. It is also illegal, except when done by a government. The *only* reason the government could do this is that it had seized monies, by a perversion of taxation, that ought never to have left the states at all, and then used these moneys to browbeat the states into doing what the Constitution specifically prohibits the federal government from doing.

Do we cry foul? Do most of us even know that this is a de facto violation of our Constitution? Are we sufficiently well educated to understand that a constitution once violated becomes malleable and tawdry? Do we care? Do we even understand anymore why this matters, why we ought to care? We do not, not after half a century of our increasingly dead public education. We no longer have the basic understanding of our rights and institutions required to protect them. But as we have already seen, liberty is not the natural state of man. It is the most fragile if lovely of blooms, and if we wish to preserve it, we must tend it lovingly. In a world where philosophy is neither valued nor discussed, where the ravings of environmental prophets of doom are the new hair shirt, the new faith, and the new inquisition, the substitute in a digital and secular world for more careful and rigorous thought, what hope is there for liberty's delicate flower?

I judge the argument in favor of understanding the corruption of social democracy so overwhelming that it hardly requires the case to be elaborately presented. It is well and fully before us, in the plainest view. The examples I have cited are illustrative, that my asseveration may be understood for what it is. No reader in a social democracy will be unwitting regarding the extent of this corruption, nor will any reader lack for ready further examples.

The questions with which the corrupt, in defense of their booty, will inevitably counter is, "Did you not vote these things?" and "Do you not enjoy the right to vote them?" Yes to both. But a right to do a thing does not make it right. These questions taken together are a sophistry and a red herring. I have a right to accost a stranger in the street and to hand him a hundred dollars. I do not have a right—by law—to accost a voter entering a polling station and to make a bargain with him that he will vote as I indicate in exchange for a hundred dollars. I can neither induce nor threaten. Our government does both, every day of every year, massively, with money seized from us under the pretense of a common good but in fact with no more than the ever more thinly veiled intent of buying votes.

There was once—I alluded to the classical free citizen—a notion, the ancient Greek notion, that a free society is underpinned by a body of free men, surely no more than a tenth of the population, who by their status, positions, and education can be considered *responsible* voters, and who can be *relied upon* to maintain liberty. The ancients did not see how this franchise could be reasonably extended to a greater number, lest it result in mob rule, itself not democratic but intrinsically tyrannical (vide the charming folk led by Danton, Robespierre, & Co.).

Even as America formulated its own notions of freedom and liberty, no one supposed the franchise could be universally extended. A requirement of property was common in the American colonies—and oft misunderstood as a broad disenfranchisement by a generation of historians writing with deliberate prejudice, the missing bit being that 90 percent of the colonials owned property. It was only with the actual founding of the United States that a pantheon of wise men saw that *all men* competent and adult—we won't herewith take up the question of women's rights or slavery, but please look these up under context of the times—should be free and enfranchised. The earlier constructs of what made a free man were to be sure somehow exclusionary, but they also represented a well-considered fear that in the hands of the masses and the mob freedom would prove tyrannical. In eighteenth- and nineteenth-century England, the king was held to be a guarantor of English liberty, somehow the more reliable for it than the unruly and emotional mob. To us, brought up in books that speak of the English king as a tyrant, this seems inexplicable. But even today, the people of many of Europe's constitutional monarchies will point to their monarch as essential to their liberty. The monarchy is a point of stability, a head of state not too tainted by political machinations, a person considered by long inheritance to have only the nation's interest at heart. A striking example would be Spain, whose King Juan-Carlos surely—by the common accord of all parties—has been indispensable to the nation's liberty and its transition from dictatorship to democracy. It has been oft said that the best form of government is a benign autocracy. No doubt it is so, the devil being to find one that remains benign; it conducts us to Churchill's insight that democracy is the very worst form of government, save all the others.

If we adjudge social democracy the best we can do, how might we take the corruption from it? Not easily. It would require that the people come to vote against their own near-term financial interests, understanding that the correction in their democracy would ultimately more than recompense them for their trouble. Do we think we can find a majority to vote against the near-term financial interest? The reader may be more optimistic than I. Practically speaking, any chance? Maybe. Either a great crisis comes upon us, forcing us to review everything from the ground up, to cause a kind of revolution; or an alternate model succeeds better than we, outpaces us, and makes us jealous to copy it. What if, for example, China keeps its taxes low and its growth high, in due course surpassing our own prosperity? It might goad us.

Absent these, I fear that no incremental diminution of the corruption, sui generis, is likely. Term limits came and went. Who was going to vote for them? The fat backsides who sit so comfortably ensconced and fed in our legislatures? Budget caps came and went. Same problem: who was going to vote for them? Pigs rarely go to empty troughs. The founders, we must admit, did a fine job of crafting our institutions. It never occurred to them that anyone could ever be so mad as to enlarge the state as it has been. They protected us from much through our institutions. Had they imagined the madness to come, they would surely have inscribed a *constitutional limitation* to the size of the state, perhaps a simple limit to taxation. That, in fact, is what is required. But it now would mean finding a majority to vote against the accretion of favors they value for themselves but reproach in their neighbors. It ain't likely.

The mischief in our gargantuan states is that the wants overwhelm the needs, and the interests behind the wants try to have us take them for needs. The result is inevitably the same: a restraint upon liberty and a consequential constraint upon prosperity. We become subject to the "Tyrants of the Wants," busybodies whose inclinations lead them to thrust their personal causes upon us and who, by their energy in promoting these causes, bend us to their wills. We do not see it coming, and by our early indifference, we allow them to build their fortress in our midst. By the time we realize the thing, the fortress is unassailable.

In my small town, a historically prosperous town, we always enjoyed town beaches and a town ski hill, staffed by volunteers and equipped by donations, with the town budget for parks and recreation reckoned at a few hundred dollars for "burgers and dogs" the Fourth of July. Today, this budget has grown to nearly half a million dollars. What did we get? We still have the same beaches, although they are now less accessible than they were—safety, don't you know—and the same ski hill, but everything is staffed by an ever-metastasizing parks and recreation bureaucracy, with all the equipment of course now purchased at town expense. I surely do not have to explain that the bureaucracy has a long shopping list for us each year. But do we get more for our money? Or do we principally fund a self-serving bureaucracy? The second box is the one with the check in it. This, a small example at a local level, is what happens at the national level on a vast scale, throughout the social democracies of the world. There is no one to say no, and by the time the need for the no is apparent, it's too late to say it.

The corruption of social democracy by massive state spending, organized principally with the purpose of buying votes to enable the incumbent to remain in power, is a reality of our stupid world. No one has yet shown that you can fix it. Ibn Khaldūn, the fourteenth-century Arab philosopher and historian had already then noted that, "In the beginning of empires the taxes are low and the revenues are high, but at the end the taxes are high and the revenues are low."

Chapter 3
The Flag of Death

Into the valley of Death
Rode the six hundred …
Theirs not to ask the reason why,
Theirs but to do and die …
—Alfred Lord Tennyson, "The Charge of the Light Brigade"

Victorians could not decently have been accused of having been pacifists or cowards. Nonetheless, Tennyson rather sums it all up; we die for the flag. We rarely ask why. And when we do ask, we are vilified. How dare we be anything less than patriotic? But it's under this flag of death that so many young men have died. Are we so sure it was all as purposeful as it was made out to be?

One of the most natural parts of the human condition, and the most deadly, is the notion of tribe. We belong to a tribe, and woe to the truly free man who says he does not. He becomes universally despised. Again the poet, now Scott, speaks: "Breathes there a man with soul so bare that he cannot say this is my own, my native land?" Against this primitive tribalism came—briefly—the Enlightenment, and a Benjamin Franklin who carefully declared, "Where there is freedom, there is my country."

We don't vilify Franklin—we revere him—but had he lived in the

America of George Bush *fils*, be assured he would have been excoriated and despised. He was a man with good knees. He didn't genuflect before any flag but liberty's. Neither did his compatriots. Their cause was freedom, not country. They were so little convinced of the virtues of country that when it came time to form one, they could not find any unanimity among themselves. They *feared* the notion of country. They had studied the tragedy and mayhem of countries throughout history. When finally they did come to create a country, their instinct was to make it as weak and subservient to the people as possible: the Articles of the Confederation, which were ultimately so weak as to create a government that could neither function nor hold itself together. When they thereafter embarked upon a stronger union, it was only with great apprehension, and the nature of that union was vigorously debated with one overwhelming concern: that the new nation should never take the people's liberty. Well, it worked for a time. And when ultimately it failed—as probably history fated it to fail—it was because of the resurgence of tribalism.

America, a nation of free men who put themselves above country—the only way to be free—developed a sense of tribe. John Kennedy's words, so often quoted to us as noble words, were exactly *wrong:* "Ask not what your country can do for you, but what you can do for your country." This is the martial music of serfs and slaves and knaves throughout all history! Free men desire their country to serve *them,* as a nation constituted in liberty—a liberty that can only ever be individual and never collective—for the purpose of protecting and maintaining their freedoms. Thus came we to the logic common to all tribes—you are either with us or against us, the death knell of liberty since time began.

In a sense, it was the Civil War that sealed the thing. Excepting upon the matter of slavery, the wrong side won. There were two American visions of nationhood: one—that of the founders—a federation in which the states would maintain their supremacy in order to ensure their citizens' liberties; the other the classical view of the nation-state built around a strong central government. Had the American

Confederacy prevailed, ours would be a very different nation today, or—more likely—there would be two nations. The CSA, very much more free than the other, would live side by side with the USA. Or perhaps the two sides would have reconciled after all, the CSA yielding on slavery—a dying institution even then—but the USA accepting a more federal view of the union. That federal view would surely have served us better than what we got.

Switzerland alone among the nations of the earth has reasonably maintained its citizens' liberties across the centuries through an adamantine attachment to federalism.

Power has an inherent life of its own—a DNA, if you will—that wants it to grow. No power is immune from this. Thus, the instinct of the founders to divide the power was exactly correct. In the Swiss *federal state*—the official name of Switzerland is the Helvetic Confederation—the cantons are supreme, as indeed our states were intended to be. Bern, the capital of this federal state, has certain designated and limited prerogatives—foreign policy being one for the obvious reason—but beyond these, it is all about the cantons. It should surprise no one that over time (and it's not a bad stretch of time since 1291) the cantons have arrogated to themselves increasing power over their citizens—powers which no Swiss free citizen would have accepted only a century ago. Perhaps it was the villages that ought to have been supreme. The more power is divided and local, the better it is for the individual. The more it is concentrated and national, the worse it goes for liberty.

In the United States, it is only two generations past that there remained a vigorous debate, touching almost all issues, about states' rights. The socialist faction in the nation (a term by which I intend a neutral economic designation and not a brand) sought to advance their agenda broadly—nationally—and thus, having for a time the ascendancy, managed to associate states' rights with segregation and to put it in bad odor. Those who still believed in American federalism were caught wrong-footed; they were surely wrong—those among them who favored segregation—morally and legally, but correct regarding the matter of states' rights. The subjugation of the states to the will of the national government profoundly affected the liberty of the American citizen.

There is no conceivable way to regain the supremacy of the states over the national government. The citizens have been bought and hog-tied. We will not find a governor of either party with the cojones to tell Washington off. If such a creature existed, we would already have heard from him. He would be unelectable today, with the people in his state—themselves bought and hog-tied by Washington—fearing for all their national booty. The courage to go it alone no longer resides in the American spine. But imagine this: a governor of courage who would make a stand, who would obtain the support of his legislature to prevent, by law, the remittance of tribute—taxes—to the national government by any person real or legal within his state. And this prohibition would stand until such time as the national government acted to restore the legitimate rights of the state—to return without strings to the state at least such monies as the state contributes to the national government.

Implausible? Absolutely. So, how might it be achieved? Rather easily, in fact: the collection of taxes from the citizens of each state must be undertaken *solely* by their home state, and such contribution as might be due to the national government must be made by that state, not by the individual citizen. This was the federalist intention—and the loss of it a first great crack in freedom's bell! The national government can easily intimidate the individual, but far less so the fifty states. This is how the Swiss have done it, with the national government requiring the assent of the cantons for its business. It is always easier for a man to have a voice in a smaller group.

As we have ceded the sovereignty and supremacy of the states, we have transferred our notion of tribe from the state to the national warlord. Our tribe is no longer Tennessee, New Hampshire, Texas, or Oregon. It is America. History teaches us that the larger the entity, the more authoritarian it will be, the more it will be tempted by foreign adventures, and the more it will kill its young men under the flag of death.

It is inconceivable that one of the greatest strategic errors in America's history, and surely one of its most immoral acts, the utterly unwarranted attack on Iraq in 2003, could have occurred if the fifty states had been ascendant. There would have been a long and tough debate, and the truth that there was no cause or justification for such an adventure would have made itself known. The toll of this extraordinary barbarism is not yet known, but to date, it approaches five thousand American deaths and well over one hundred thousand civilian deaths in a country we attacked for the hell of it, just because we could and a few guys over beers thought it'd be cool to do. In a historical context, this will come to be seen little differently from Genghis Khan in winter quarters planning the next season's rape and pillage. And the security we mistakenly sought through this wanton war—because the target was easy—was entirely lost, with precious time and resources taken from the battle that did matter (that in the tribal lands of the Afghan-Pakistani border) with a punishing recession thrown in for good measure.

Americans long saw their nation as moral and long encouraged it to be fundamentally isolationist—indeed, it was George Washington's recommendation to future generations—in the pursuit of its own happiness, while suffering others to get on with theirs as they saw fit. "Be neither too great a friend nor too great an enemy to any foreign power, for both enslave." There is nothing to be improved upon in Washington's admonition even now. But as we lost our federalist state and the national warlord consolidated his domination of us, as ever more our gaze was directed to the majesty on the Potomac, the more we became inclined to foreign glory and adventure, the *via victoris* of Caesar, Timur, and Napoleon. Thus did we take what we intended for our own domestic morality—our own right—and sought to impose it upon others, entirely outside our right. In the nineteenth century, the nation's first century, our foreign adventures were connected to our own borders. We recognize today that some of these adventures were, strictly considered—ahem—extra-legal, but they at least had a cause that was largely sui generis: the expansion of the eager and rambunctious young nation across a largely empty continent. As the twentieth century dawned, things changed. Already one president, with a self-image at times in Caesar's mold, had signaled to the world that the United States would be a world power: Theodore Roosevelt. The world-circling mission of the Great White Fleet was tantamount to a "We're here" declaration by the young republic. The thing wasn't done yet, and the prudence and traditional isolationism of the country reasserted themselves. There was *no* desire for the nation to enter the Great War in Europe in 1914. Had the Kaiser only been a little wiser, it would have been the easiest thing to keep the United States out of it. Who knows how this might have influenced the course of events as the world pursued its terrible fate in the score of years after Versailles? It is always the same: for want of a nail, a shoe is lost; for want of a shoe, a horse is lost …

Even after WWI the nation—by an older understanding but now unwisely—dismantled its armed forces, giving proof yet then that the isolationist impulse remained dominant. Could a greater engagement have saved the world from the horrors of WWII? Surely yes, but that engagement could not fairly have been asked of the United States. It was for England and France to act. The will wasn't there. Clemenceau knew it. Churchill knew it. But the First World War had exacted such a terrible toll, had taken an entire generation from their parents, that no one could find the heart for yet another war, and no one wanted to listen to more sober voices. Churchill, asked what WWII might be called, replied "the unnecessary war." Marshall Foch had disdained Versailles as not a peace but an armistice for twenty years. Exactly. It was also the First World War that seeded the ground for that most monstrous of tyrannies, the Soviet one over the Russian people. That bit of madness—an urban-atheistic religious cause born in the excited minds of a band of rich kids and intellectuals—cost Russia tens of millions of lives, cost the Russian people four generations, and cost the world more than a hundred million lives and untold misery.[3]

We spoke in Chapter 1 of Mancur Olson's thesis of roving and

---

3   The impulse did not die, and can be found again now, but that will be for another chapter. Professor Ian Plimer is the source for the term and the notion of an urban-atheistic religion, to which I refer.

stationary bandits. These are tribes. The tribe engenders loyalty, because it provides protection, identity, and opportunity. These are rational benefits. So long as the tribal leader brings value to the tribal members— safety, food, fulfillment—we can say he performs a useful function. It is not true that all men can stand on their own feet, and thus— regrettably—the tribal leader seems a necessity. Stay with me on this. We all know that there are good and bad leaders. In one interpretation the good leader is the successful leader—Caesar or Napoleon … or Hitler. In another interpretation, the good leader is the benign visionary, rarer than the first type, who brings peace and prosperity to his tribe. At times the one has elements of the other. The problem with the first type, the successful one, is that he exists on a slippery slope. How many of these began by bringing blessings to their tribe but as their power grew came to the megalomania that power so often engenders? How they then abused their leadership to drive their tribe to flag and glory … and death!

This is not an easy thing to counter. We seem to have an inborn need to win. And if we cannot ourselves win, individually, then let us win through the collective, our team. We can see the vast enthusiasm of sports fans as all good fun or as a (sensible) substitute for war: "our tribe" against "their tribe." When power is misused, the dividing line between sport and national necessity is blurred. Throughout history charismatic leaders have misused their hold over their tribes, their people, to engage in sport on a grand scale: the slaughter of the opposing tribe. The examples are so numerous as not to require insistence: all the warlords and kings and emirs and chieftains who would return to their castles or encampments for the winter season, only to plot the next summer's mayhem, basically the "away games." These were contests of rape, pillage, and death—high entertainment for the tribe, around which an entire structure of society was built: rank, prestige, nobility, honor, chivalry, wealth, arms … and death.

Under the tsars of Russia, a nobleman had two courses open to him: arms or administration. Either way, his life was the tsar's. He was a slave in a gilded cage offered all the privileges and honors and wines and beautiful women of the world in exchange for his life, the property of the tsar. When Alexander II manumitted the serfs in 1861, he omitted to free the nobles. No tears for that, but if we take a step back and look at the thing for what it was, we can see a society structured on service and obeisance to flag and country and warlord. If we take yet another step back, what do we see? A tribe. Roving bandits who became successful enough to become stationary at the fortresses of Kiev, Moscow, and St. Petersburg. Sufficient wealth to reward the best warriors—and through them their offspring across innumerable rather useless generations, exemplifying the essence of hereditary privilege. The justification for hereditary privilege, as opposed to merit, is clear: it keeps the power center of the tribe deeply loyal to the warlord. They are interdependent.

A stark example of how things go wrong—Ibn Khaldūn's insight again—can be found in the story of the Ottoman Empire, which for the first three centuries after its founding was surely the most enlightened regime the world had ever seen, a remarkable meritocracy preserved, perhaps, by the fact that the tribe, the empire, had remained a roving one. But in time the accretions of power and privilege proved too seductive to resist: magnificent palaces, the finest foods and silks, a comfort and ease of rare quality, and the most nubile girls brought from across the dominions, ready to hand. Those who had earned—truly earned—their daily bread in productive service to the tribe, to the empire, lost their vigor and allowed luxury to sap their strength. They could well afford to buy others to do the fighting for them. They could be safe in their ease while minions and hirelings ran the place. Privilege was no longer earned; it was handed down. And thus the Ottoman Empire, which had served its varied peoples so well for so long, became fat, stupid, and debauched. Power and position became the currencies, oppression the vehicle, taxes the fuel. By the late nineteenth century, the Ottoman Empire had simply collapsed of its own weight, obese and effete.

It isn't well seen to speak of Adolf Hitler but to condemn him, yet he is a leader worthy of our study, if only to understand how things so easily go seriously wrong. The Germans, as Julius Caesar had noted two millennia before, are a tough, proud, and warlike people. It is a mistake to wound a tiger, and the wretched Treaty of Versailles assured that the wound remained opened and salted. A Hitler would have come forth under such circumstances in any robust tribe, wherever upon the earth it might have been. What did he promise? Food, work, pride, success, fulfillment, confidence. And vengeance. Anything wrong with this list? Yes, the mad vengeance. How many peoples—how many tribes—would not have put vengeance on the list? Right. Had the tiger's wound been salved—the very thing done for Japan and Germany after the Second World War—it would have been far wiser, and Hitler would not have become the *democratically elected* chancellor of Germany. But he did. And then what did he do? Almost all of the good things on the list. That is inevitably overlooked in much of what we read. But then came the mad vengeance, with the most tragic consequences for the German people, their neighbors, and the world.

In spite of what we are told in our schoolbooks, in the course of mankind's awful and savage history, Hitler was only a middling tyrant. Genghis Khan made it his pleasure to wipe out—exterminate, not move—all of the peoples in a broad swath from Mongolia to Europe, over five thousand miles. Why? So his horses could have a great grassy plain upon which to run and to graze as he plundered ever further west. The Mongols stacked the heads of the slaughtered in great columns, 100,000 skulls to a column. Tamurlane thought the lesson exemplary and did the same as his hordes swept west from central Asia to the Mediterranean. Stalin, a man whose madness drove him to destroy more than twenty million of his own citizens, had only one object in his life: his personal power. Upon that altar were all those lives sacrificed, and untold more wasted. Mao Zhedong, in the East, took China and made it his private madhouse, its teeming millions his slaves—his adoring slaves, if the accounts of the time are to be believed. So he killed a hundred million, plus or minus. So what? As the communists liked to say, you can't make an omelet without breaking a few eggs. These madmen, Stalin and Mao, created cults in which they made themselves gods. They took the First Commandment for their own. They had to tear down other religions or they could not be the one god. And what of the instruments of the insanity? Flag. Country. Patriotism. And death. Yes, death, which is never far when flag, country, and patriotism are abroad.

This terrible cycle of tribe-flag-loyalty has, through the course of man's history, often killed one-quarter of the male population. Yes, *one-quarter,* one out of four men. We sometimes wonder from our Western perch at societies wherein men may take more than one wife. There was a very good reason for it. There were not enough men to go around, and it was the only way to look after the tribe's women: to feed them, to house them, and to protect them. Now the tricky bit.

It is not true that all war is unjustified. Pacifism is a luxury of the secure. There are perfectly valid reasons for war: to protect or gain liberty, to defend one's home or land, to keep oneself from starving, to prevent a neighbor who is making aggressive noises—credible aggressive noises—from acting upon his promise. Most wars throughout history have not been fought for these reasons. They were games of flag and glory, the boyish ambitions of chieftains and peoples with time on their hands and dreams to live.

There is however—and this is the subtle bit—a continuum between justifiable war and frivolous war. We like to think that our social democracies do not go frivolously to war. We don't plan next summer's crusade simply because we haven't anything else to do. Or do we? The American response—initially—in Afghanistan to the 9/11 incident seemed justified. In fact almost all of the world's peoples understood it, condoned it, and wished America well. If such incidents as 9/11 came to be commonplace, everyone might be affected. Thus, with the exception of a few pacifists whom we can respect but with whom we cannot agree, we had a legitimate casus belli. But for the sporting crowd in the White House, egged on by cynical agents of a foreign power (Israel), that wasn't really enough. We needed to whup 'em, to teach 'em a lesson, to show the world what our team could do. Do we remember now with any embarrassment that "shock and awe" schoolboy bluster? We should, but with much more than embarrassment—with profound embarrassment and shame. There were—I remember it—absolutely awful scenes of our troops going off to the crusade in Iraq, football game scenes missing only the cheerleaders in spangly tights, where troops overjuiced and overvitamined exclaimed joyfully, "I'm pumped!" "I'm ready for 'em!" "We'll fly our flag high and show 'em!" "This flag don't run!" Right. Now many are dead. So are over one hundred thousand civilians, whose blood is on our hands.

The decent men who went off to war for us in 1941 weren't "pumped." They were sober, quiet, and determined. They knew theirs would be a tough, grim job. They knew some wouldn't return. They also knew they went for a decent purpose, not to kill if it could be helped—certainly not wantonly and unnecessarily—but to resist militaristic empires, whose ambitions put the world, *and us*, at risk. It was done reluctantly, but it had to be done, so it was. The dogs of war ought never to be unleashed, save reluctantly. That WWII generation of soldiers came from the western mountains, from the farms of the Great Plains, from the cities of the coasts, from rich and poor, from black and white, and all marched to a war they had neither chosen nor desired—not to the music of glory but to the call of necessity. All honor to them.

In Iraq, through the unwisdom of some and the cynicism and ambition of others, the United States broke its moral compact and used a professional army to engage in an away game whose purpose was, except to the puppet masters in Israel, to even the score. We forgot the lesson of Sun-Tzu: before setting out upon revenge, dig two graves. We chose Iraq not because we had any cause to, but because Saddam Hussein was convenient, a bit of a buffoon, surely a strongman and a "bad guy" to his own people, but who threatened us not at all, nor could he have. (Dictators are rarely suicidal. Job One is staying in power and preserving their thrones. Attacking an overwhelmingly stronger power is not a proven way to achieve this. Someone might think this through as regards Iran.)

The (initial) reaction of the American people was neither true to

America's values nor worthy of a good people: they gloried in their flag and their arms. Later, the faction promoting this view intimidated those who began to doubt, acting in many respects as Brown Shirts in Nazi Germany. They waved the colors in everyone's face and beat the angry drum of patriotism. As George Bush had declared, "If you aren't with us, you're against us." If we look back on the films of Leni Riefenstahl, the films of the Nuremberg rallies, and just squint a bit, what do we see? Eager endless columns of the faithful. Nazi banners everywhere. Eagles atop great pillars. The massed voices of a hundred thousand, all crying out for the victory of their tribe, burning for that victory, anxious to give their lives for it, impatient to die. That is the force of flag and glory, the terrible force that through some siren song to our primitive ear calls us to battle ... and death.

George Washington was no pacifist, and no man could ever have said he wanted for courage. Yet he warned us against foreign entanglements and surely prayed his country would never engage in distant adventures. It was not the purpose of the United States to do so, a nation conceived in liberty *for liberty*. There is a great distinction between the liberty of the Enlightenment and the "fight for freedom" of the Iraq War, a fight that in fact has nothing to do with freedom, and through which the American people gave up their fundamental freedoms, somehow in freedom's name. This was and is snake oil.

In Orwell's *1984* we learned to be wary of language misused, only repeating the stark admonitions of the prophet Isaiah. In the America of the early 2000s, the word "freedom" ceased to carry its proper meaning, rooted in liberty, and took on the same sort of perversion it had in the Soviet dictatorship and all the other communist tyrannies of the twentieth century. It was code for "our policy." The "fight for freedom" had nothing to do with freedom; it was about signing on to a jingoistic and aggressive foreign policy, cynically egged on by the administration's remora-like éminence grise, Israel, and seeking a unilateral approach to national life that had nothing to do with our liberty.

Liberty implies—no, requires and is defined by—tolerance for many opinions. America for a time became entirely intolerant, led by angry voices of absolutism. These voices could not accept that there might be any opinion save their own, and they preyed upon families with sons and daughters serving in the armed forces, equating any deviation from their war purpose as a betrayal of the troops, as cowardice and treason. We can understand the sentiments of families with soldiers "out there fighting." We can doubt that none of them doubted. We can suspect that they were cowed and made quiet, as Red Sox fans at Yankee Stadium. That's all it was in fact: our team against their team. And death.

The flag of which Francis Scott Key wrote was not the flag of country—it was the flag of liberty. It isn't the same thing. The flag under which the troops endured at Valley Forge was not the flag of country—it was the flag of liberty. The cause to which the founders rallied wasn't the cause of country—it was the cause of liberty. In each case this was the liberty of the Enlightenment, the liberty of Locke and Mill and Jefferson. It had nothing to do with country. If anything, it feared country. To understand this requires us to read philosophy, to comprehend distinctions and nuances, to know something of the awful history of the world, to have a passing acquaintance with Plato's *Republic*, to have the memory of tyranny in our family's bones, and to yearn for the liberty of the individual, entirely apart from the collective. Indeed, there is no such thing as collective liberty; liberty is, as we have said, always individual.

In pre-WWII Germany the soldiers took a *Fahneneid*, the "flag oath." Thus is the world. Flag. Oath. Loyalty. Country. Death. There is no honor in wanton murder. A country conceived in liberty, a country whose entire purpose is liberty, can only hide its head in shame.

I do not think the founders would have recited the Pledge of Allegiance. Their purpose was liberty, to which they gladly pledged their lives, their fortunes, and their sacred honors.

Postscript:

I have had personal experience trying to make the distinction between the flag and liberty, and it isn't easy. It incites violent opinions. Yet, in a free country, it ought to be a hallmark of freedom that different opinions can be voiced and fairly heard. But when discussion touches the flag, things become tribal and basic very quickly. In the time of the administration of George W. Bush, a loud and all but totalitarian faction made the flag their sword and shield, in support of a foreign policy many—ultimately the majority—thought very wrong. These goose-stepping ideologues wrapped themselves in the flag and cried "treason!" at anyone who did not goose-step with them. They cynically used the understandable sentiments of families of servicemen and women to defend themselves.

I would put it to those who may consider the flag an object of veneration that they ask themselves whether they have ever heard, anywhere at any time, of a "flag of oppression." I think they will have to admit they have not. In even the most horrendous dictatorships, it is always "the flag of freedom." It is just that freedom doesn't mean the same thing everywhere. We must be careful when revering "the flag of freedom"; no dictator, no regime, no administration has ever called it otherwise. It serves a purpose so, as a rallying point for tribal members around the tribal banner. But free men fight only for freedom, with liberty as their only rallying point, not the flag.

The flag is an icon, and dictators have known it and used it so since the beginning of man's time in this world. Beneath the colors, beneath the banner of tribe and country, untold millions have died, their only cause the warlord's cause, the dictator's cause, the demagogue's cause, who in turn had as his only purpose his own glory, his own ambition. Under liberty all may claim the flag theirs—whether they assent or dissent—for the flag does no more than represent their liberty. When a flag comes to mean other than liberty, it becomes a danger to liberty and the icon of demagoguery and totalitarianism.

Chapter 4
Superstition

Superstition is the enemy of enlightenment. We are surrounded by superstition. Nothing is more primitive. Nothing is more natural.

It would seem that man requires spirituality and will, for the want of it, invent it. Voltaire had much to say regarding this, and we won't say here what has already been better said. What, on the other hand, we can examine is what I believe has been a return to an early medieval form of superstition, surprisingly—or maybe not—in our digital age. In stating this, we must take note of yet another distinction concerning superstition: it has affected different parts of our world, different cultures, differently. In some way all have been touched.

I think it fair to say that up to the Second World War, thus roughly through the middle of the twentieth century, the world was as it had always been. From the Dark Ages, we entered upon medieval times; from the late medieval era, we found the Renaissance; from the Renaissance, the Enlightenment; from the Enlightenment, pari passu science; from science, the Industrial Revolution; from the Industrial Revolution, social revolution; then, from our sense of being masters of fate, the arrogance of atheism in various guises; and from atheism, superstition. Thus, until mid-century God was in his heaven, however the peoples of the earth understood that. Nothing happens without rivulets becoming streams and streams rivers, and no river disperses into the sea all of a sudden without trace of itself. In the story of man, it is no less so. Perhaps, socially speaking, one of the most meaningful rivers of the last two and a half centuries has been that of revolution: the American Revolution, which was about liberty; the French Revolution, which began about liberty but which wasn't long born before becoming the torture of egalitarianism; and the Russian Revolution, which only very briefly pretended to be about liberty and then became the dictatorship of the proletariat, the monstrous invention of energetic idlers in a bloody quest for absolute power. But one led to the other.

The American revolutionaries made their obeisance to Providence but put a certain space between it and them. The French revolutionaries thought to set aside Providence, wrapping it in a fabric of blather and sophistry. The Russian revolutionaries denied Providence altogether in order to replace it with themselves. Thus it came full circle: if not Providence in one form, then another. But Providence in the proper sense isn't so easily replaced. It is vastly more subtle and finely crafted than that. The copy only resembles the original if one is satisfied with rough pottery in the place of porcelain. Our dialogue will not be about faith and God. It will be philosophical and inquisitive. It will depend upon an understanding of nuance, not belief. We return to man's apparent absolute need for spirituality.

Spirituality is complex. It touches our souls, whether we hold this to be God given or simply a godless definition of self. It represents in some way our best, who we are, who we know ourselves to be, what we are doing in this world, the Big Why. Atheist and believer alike share this sense of being more than stone, more than a clever Meccano set with complex wiring, more than an automaton of chemistry and physics. Some hold that we are no more than this, but do not act upon it; they represent it intellectually but are unable to absorb it emotionally. We are arrogant. We are more than stone. Whether acting under God or proclaiming ourselves gods, we have a high opinion of ourselves.

I have always had the feeling that atheists somehow get a free ride in a society largely comprising believers. They enjoy the luxury of their liberation while never straying far from the security of their birth. It is akin to coastal sailing—always near a safe harbor. The atheist takes for his own the values, the morality, and the purpose of the society that surrounds him, but denies their source. There is nothing dishonest or reproachable in this. A man can only feel what he feels. The dishonesty is in the other way: feigning, as so many have, their obedience to God while acting to the contrary. If we can hope for some ultimate reckoning, we can hope for a severe one for those who do this. In private life, it is hypocrisy; in public life, demagoguery. We return to our thesis.

A plant is one with the soil from which it grows. It cannot be otherwise unless it is tumbleweed. The soil makes it, succors it, sees it bloom, and takes it back for itself when it dies. A man is a plant. He cannot just cut himself loose from the culture that bore him and reappear, *deus ex machina*, upon an unknown stage. Monsters like Stalin and Mao were of their cultures, subject to centuries of habit, manner, and thought. Saints—metaphorically speaking—like Henri IV, Marcus Aurelius, and Washington were of their cultures. They spoke the language of their fathers; they thought in the manner of the grammar to which they were born; they understood the world by their own cultures before they chose their paths. This is why I think it right to say that the atheist, in a society largely of believers, however varied their beliefs, gets a free ride. He is not able to be, using a mathematical notion, an absolute atheist. He has quotation marks around himself, not brackets. I would suggest that this intuition can hold until the majority come to see themselves in a secular light. At that point, the safe harbor recedes. And, I believe, this now increasing distance between us and port explains the renewal of superstition in our twenty-first-century world.

Faced with ever more astonishing science (we are told that the sum knowledge of man doubles every seven years), we believe ever more fantastic things: rumors, false science, bizarre cults, and broadly held but absolutely unsupported ideas.

As the Western nations came out of the Second World War in possession of the enormous medical advances the war brought, we had a sense that medicine had become a reliable science—that doctors could be believed, that we either knew or almost knew or soon would know everything there was to know. We trusted. We submitted to surgeries in which we believed. We took medicines whose worth was—we were confident—proven by science. It took a generation to understand it wasn't quite so, to come to the reflection of the wise physician that our knowledge is small … and even then, suspect. Disappointed that we hadn't found the key to physical immortality, we turned against good science and invented pseudoscience, a form of witchcraft as primitive as chicken bones poked through earlobes. And we institutionalized this pseudoscience through political correctness and public policy, these at times being one and the same.

In 2009 the Brown government in the United Kingdom sacked their director of drug policy, a professor by the infelicitous name of Nutt, because he spoke the truth. Simple as that. Professor Nutt contravened public policy with honest science, openly stating what is reliably known: that certain currently illegal drugs, such as marijuana and ecstasy, are objectively less dangerous than alcohol or riding a horse. But of course this ran up against the myths perpetrated by latter- day moralists and could not be allowed to stand. Professor Nutt, in his government's remarkably bold-faced admission, was fired for disagreeing with public policy. I think the exact words were "failing to uphold," but the clear meaning was inescapable: we have a public policy, knowledge and science be damned, and you will toe the line … or else. Galileo would have understood and would likely have been unsurprised at our lack of progress over four centuries.

Two problems pervade our society's approach to psychotropic substances. The first is scientific: much of what is said, repeated, and taken for true is false. The second is fundamental to the rights of man: the government has been granted a right it simply does not morally have. Regarding the first, we learn that psychotropic substances are life destroying, instantly addictive, and a slippery slope to hell. Shades of Demon Rum and Prohibition! In fact, many illicit psychotropic substances are far more benign than their readily accepted alternatives: booze, tranquilizers, amphetamines, serotonin inhibitors, and assorted alternative therapies. The supposition that heroin, for example, is fatally addictive was categorically dispelled when hundreds of thousands of soldiers returned to the United States from the war in Vietnam, having used heroin, and never again touched the stuff once they were back home. Observation tells us that addiction is far more a psychological disease than a physical one.

Alcohol, for a small proportion of the population, becomes a need—a desperate need, an addiction. For most of us, it just doesn't. Tobacco, nicotine really, seems to readily create a dependency. Some can smoke occasionally and stop at will. Others cannot. Yet recreational substances whose effects are no greater than or not much different from alcohol and tobacco will land us in jail—in some states, for an extraordinarily long time. Why? Whose business is it that we use such substances? Why does anyone care? What is the underlying science?

When we consider the harm the attempted prohibition of recreational drugs has wrought … when we contemplate the shattered lives, the waste of funds on a scale that defies accounting or belief, the corruption of justice and of the police, and the transformation of society … and then consider alongside these the small, not to say puny, true effects of these substances, we have to wonder if we have gone mad. There is less *scientific* debate about recreational drugs than the popular imagination believes. These drugs are in their majority no more, and often less, dangerous than alcohol or tobacco, but we have decreed a false science regarding them to support what is only a moral judgment. Yet, when charlatan physicians—oh, to be sure, licensed by the state—prescribe deadly cocktails of drugs to their patients in pursuit of some sort of relief for varied ills, we take it for medicine. There is, locally to me, such a physician, a quack who has built a practice as the good doctor who brings relief to the elderly. Where he ought to have told his patients that with age comes certain aches and infirmities, he prescribed potent drugs whose only proper use is temporary relief from serious affliction, not as long-term palliatives.

Of course his patients felt better at first; so would they have with morphine. Over time their bodies succumbed, with many dying wretched deaths—enfeebled, fragile, and visually transformed beyond decency or recognition. Nurses spoke to me of what they saw, that this doctor "did this to one patient after another." If someone belongs in jail to rue his sins, it is he! But no, what he does is not only legal, but it earns him a respected place in the community. Superstition? Yes. What has the sanction of public policy is legal, and what does not is not.

One reads that among America's vast prison population, something like half of the inmates are serving time for drug related offenses. More than 50 percent of these are guilty of a crime that had no victim, and the other 50 percent would not have had a victim but for the illegality—by law but by no other reason—of recreational drugs. Who has the most direct interest in keeping such drugs illegal—in fact in assuring the most determined and protracted war on drugs? The drug dealers! That much is evident, incontrovertibly reposing on solid economic law. Were we ever to legalize recreational drugs, the drug dealers and all of the violence and burden and death that go with their traffic would end. If one could buy such drugs at the local pharmacy, the local liquor store, or the local tobacconist, the drug dealer's entire business would collapse, and his network of crime with it. If ever we wonder where the antidrug money comes from, we have no further to look: any dealer interested in the future of his business will contribute generously, however veiled, to campaigns vociferously advocating prohibition. Nothing better for business!

We have forgotten the lessons of our rather recent past: the Volstead Act, commonly known as Prohibition. No single act of law ever did more for the creation of crime in the United States. Indeed, organized crime traces its origin to Prohibition. In spite of the moralists among us—trading in their own problems, perspectives, and religious views—certain activities remain attractive to us that no law and no punishment will stop. One of these is surely a need for a sort of space and relaxation, found by some in psychotropic substances. Another is gambling. Yet another is prostitution. Why do we bother banning these? Myths and hokum: superstition!

We have discussed recreational drugs. We have spoken of the false science repeated as gospel truth that underpins much of what is said about them. We have seen the example of Professor Nutt, fired from his post in a modern society in 2009 because he failed to lie in accord with government policy. Professor Nutt was widely supported by the scientific community in the United Kingdom, to no avail. The brouhaha soon passed.

The ills of drugs are mainly psychological ills, not dissimilar from any irresistible need.

Food: if we define a drug by its addictive potential, food is a far worse addiction of our rich societies, judging by our relentlessly increasing obesity.

Gambling: unrestrained, it's a terrible thing, but otherwise only an entertainment. Restraint, however, must come in the form of self-discipline, not law. By what right does the state instruct me that I may not put what I have earned at risk, whether for pleasure or gain? Nine out of ten new businesses fail and often take life savings with them. The odds are frankly better in Las Vegas or Monte Carlo. Ought we to make the gamble of founding a business illegal? Of course we know of the life-destroying effects of compulsive gambling. The reality is that this is a psychological affliction, and it touches only a small number among us. It has nothing to do with recreational gambling, which draws millions of fans with no worse effect than—on sum—that they lose a little more than they win, the odds of the house dictating as much.

Prostitution: might as well ban sex. We argue before the Supreme Court that in the matter of abortion, a woman has the right to her own body. Set aside whether we consider that argument just or unjust; it is made. And upon it, our society—in its majority—has acquiesced and in some way has come to accept abortion. So, a woman has a right to her body, even when a primitive would say that there is a second body involved, but she hasn't the right to sell her own body for sexual use. On the other hand, she does have the right to become a masseuse, in some states by official license—and to provide massages whose therapeutic purpose is principally pleasure. I do not refer to sexual massage. What does she do with her body? She uses it to give pleasure. What does a prostitute do?

In all of the above—drugs, gambling, prostitution—we are dealing with consensual crime: crimes defined by law but not crimes per se. We tolerate the criminalization of activities that in fact cannot be suppressed. We know that sin—as some might label the above acts—comes also to cloisters and monasteries. Each is free to seek his salvation in his own way, or not, but surely is not free to impose a personal religious view upon his fellows. We may wince when we see flagellants; we may wonder at the moral hurt that drives them to this peculiar pain; but we do not interfere. We may disdain it, we may ignore it, and we may respect it, but ultimately it just isn't our business. What we don't seem to do is to condemn it.

What is the logic then of hauling away a teenager in handcuffs because—horrors!—he was found with a cigarette or smoking a joint, but standing by in awe should the same teen whip his back to blood with thorns? Which harmed him the more? Thus have we chosen our society's poisons entirely without enlightened reason. The choices are private moral choices imposed upon us by the force of the state. It explains why we are gleeful when a well-known televangelist is caught in a motel room somewhere concealing a very surprised pink French poodle. It is a small but delicious revenge. When the same—we speak of the televangelist, not the pooch—then appears tearfully before the cameras, begging forgiveness, the spectacle is nothing short of loathsome.

It is the very criminalization of consensual crime that has made the crime. Our drug czars are the grand inquisitors, our bunko squads and vice squads the goons of a modern-day inquisition. The purpose of the Inquisition was that each man and woman in the land should fear. Centuries later, Felix Dzerzhinsky was named grand inquisitor of the Soviet Union. The purpose was precisely the same: that all should be guilty, that all should fear. These are the instruments of oppression. We tolerate and condone them even as we wonder at the dark side of the Inquisition. We are missing something. The greatest terror through all time has been that which masquerades as law. Never did foreign terror—that which so exercised us after 9/11—injure and destroy and kill as the terror sponsored by law. In other states and other times, outside of the Western social democracies, internal state-sponsored terror swept millions to their destruction, all lawfully. When we are killed upon the altar of morality by our own tribe, we say amen. When we are killed upon the altar of grievance by another tribe, we shriek bloody murder. Both ways we die.

By criminalizing what is not criminal, we create a criminal class and in the process form some very bad criminals indeed. We have only to see the mayhem that follows drug gangs. *But these gangs would not exist were drugs legal.* We read that drugs pass the border not covertly; not, as we might imagine, clandestinely; not smuggled in the dark of night; but openly, in fully loaded tractor trailers. I do not think I need to detail how that can be possible. It is corruption—corruption on a massive scale, extending its tentacles throughout our police forces and into every corridor of government. Why? There is a lot of money in it. A lot. A man who is incorruptible in the face of a hundred bucks is not so in the face of ten thousand or a hundred thousand. These figures are small change to the drug barons, just so much paper with the number "20" printed on it. Like Prohibition, whose corruption reached everywhere and whose ill-judged purpose persists to this day, the war on drugs has created vast fortunes and empires of crime. And it's all based on two great misconceptions, the one scientific and the other philosophical.

Now, as the science finally can no longer be suppressed, the vested interests within the crime networks and within politics and law enforcement, all of whom depend for their lucre upon this damnable war going on forever, are responding with every weapon at their disposal. After all, their livelihoods are at risk. At least the criminals are frank about it. The politicians and the law enforcement personnel who have committed their careers to this terrible engine of destruction are *all* corrupt, either consciously taking money and favors, or—in the case of those who are more decent but less bright—unconsciously being used by the drug barons … and taking money and favors. How so? Money is contributed to an antidrug politician's campaign. Where does it come from? Who has the greatest interest to keep drugs illegal *and* has unlimited money to promote it? We are informed that the illegal drug trade is the single largest industry in the United States. Let us repeat that to ourselves so it sinks in: the illegal drug trade is the single largest industry in the nation.

Everything we do to counter the drug trade only serves the trade's purpose. To the extent that supply can be constrained, the price increases, which only increases the violence. Legalization would shut down the business at one stroke. Without any need to fear for society, we could release a great number of police officers so that they might find productive work; release at least a quarter of our prison population, whose crime was victimless and only a crime by our say-so; *close* a great number of prisons; reduce violent crime by at least a third; and not insignificantly grant to adult and presumably free citizens the right to put whatever they darn well please into themselves. After all, we're free to eat Big Macs.

While we're at it, we should legalize gambling and prostitution. Our animus toward these is a reflection of a private morality that ought not to be imposed on citizens who may be indifferent to it. The cries one can expect—that crime comes with gambling and prostitution and drugs—are only true when we criminalize what some take only for sins. That is what brings the heavies, the thugs, the pimps, the coercion, the violence, and the menace. If gambling and prostitution are not criminal, there is no crime. The gambling den suddenly becomes a bingo hall, and the prostitute's service takes on the aspect of any other service— housekeeping, window washing, whatever. I would not ask those who see these as sinful not to. It is their right. I, however, see hypocrisy as a greater sin. In the injunction commanding us to abnegate false witness, we can read a corollary against hypocrisy. But that is my private view. I would never suggest that hypocrisy be made illegal.

I once heard a commentator speak of "mom rules" and "dad rules." He wisely commented that both mom and dad rules were good rules, but that mom rules, tending to be moral injunctions, made for good recommendations but bad law; dad rules, tending to be basic and practical—"Don't play in the street; you'll be run over!"—were adaptable to law. The distinction, however couched, is a sensible one. We suffer our liberties grievous harm when we allow mom rules to become law. We see this in a frightening guise now as our social democracies, in which freedom of speech was a central tenet, deny our liberty to say certain things. It has been made illegal, punishable with imprisonment, in a number of European social democracies to deny the existence of the Holocaust. Why? Because it actually happened? We deny many historical realities. Our schoolbooks deny them, and we are made to learn it so, and to recite it so. Are we—or better yet, the hypocritical authors of these false texts—to be incarcerated for it, given fifty lashes, and excommunicated? Perhaps it is a man's view that the Holocaust did not occur, or did not occur exactly as routinely affirmed. So what? No one has to accept his view. That is the essence of free speech.

Europe isn't stopping at the imposition of one historical reality. Now there is hate speech, and that is illegal too. What is hate speech? Something that offends another? The old rule was the better: ignore harsh words; they only reflect badly upon the speaker.

Not surprisingly those advancing the view that global warming is the greatest threat to mankind since Noah's flood are floating the idea, not yet made law, that denying this unproven thesis ought to be forbidden—yes, made illegal. And they have so invaded the political and chattering classes that global warming is taught as fact and faith in schools. To express a contrary opinion is to invite the most vicious personal attacks, to ensure ostracism from the right people, and to be disdained as someone nursing an emotional disability. There is comfort in knowing that Galileo may be better company than these trendy bullies. We will speak more of this later.

For now, this: when we seek to legislate morality, we not only offend liberty, we fatally cripple it. We must choose, for the very notion of liberty implies the liberty to be right, to be wrong, to speak, or not to speak. Liberty is a whole fabric. To tear it even in small part is to rend it entirely.

We began with superstition, and to superstition we return. Take water. Yes, water. Sometime in the last couple of decades, someone decreed that a human body needed to ingest a swimming pool full of water each day to survive. The evidence was rather to the contrary, the human race having come thus far without continuous hydration. Wars were fought, mountains climbed, sweaters knitted, races run, books read, afternoons passed, flights taken, and shopping done, all—mirabile dictu—without the now ever-present water bottle. It is astonishing that anyone survived—almost as surprising as entire generations of children having made it to adulthood without bicycle helmets to find themselves no more injured than the present batch. It would be too easy to surmise that some marketing genius at Evian launched the whole thing at a Monday morning blue-sky meeting. It is true that Europeans had long imbibed the myth of bottled waters. The origin of that one is easy, and sensible enough: anyone my age or older can remember the uncertainty of potable tap water in Europe. In the Third World today, one finds bottled water everywhere. That makes sense, too, the public water supply being dicey at best. In our modern social democracies, bottled water is asinine.

If only it had ended there. It did not. It became a cult.

Who has not sat through a meeting in which some supremely irritating individual—usually in the plural—did not incessantly unscrew and screw the cap of his damned water bottle, taking more sips from the nipple than a babe suckling at its mother's breast? The water drinkers became a society, felicitating themselves on how much water they were consuming, looking to each other with coded compliments as they forced down one more gulp. Some died. Well, yes, I'm being deliberately provocative. I don't think they died in meetings, but some did die on the athletic field, from overhydration. I don't think it right to be gleeful for it, but still …

What took hold was—yet is—a water mania. This is a superstition and *nothing else*. It is true that some elderly persons lose the impulse of thirst and become dehydrated. No doubt they need to be mindful and to counter that. But anyone of normal good health will know when to drink. That's what thirst does; it tells us when to drink. What overwhelmed the media was stuff that attained lunatic levels. "You can't drink enough." "Water is nature's lubricant." "We are water." "Water keeps your skin young." It turned out that, according to the hype, water could cure heart disease, liver disease, and probably seborrhea. Would that it were so simple. Of course water does none of these, nor does it provide the spring tide of other benefits that appeared in every manner of publication and chatter—regrettably including medical journals.

Physicians who ought to have known better delivered themselves of the most fantastic and self-evidently foolish opinions. Of course they could always fall back on a bit of soft-shoe: "What we really said is that those who don't drink enough must take care to drink enough." Yeah … only that isn't what they really said. Anyone who goes back and checks will find that what was given was broad and unequivocal support for consuming unnatural quantities of water. Why? Because it was popular, because it was the regnant superstition, because it was the pap of the day, because that's what paid.

I had a manager in my employ, a jogger. He must have ground his knee joints to a fine powder. He kept *a case* of water bottles beneath his desk. He could not walk anywhere in our small office without his bottle in hand, taking no less than a sip per minute. It would have been easier to come to work on a gurney with a hydrating IV stuck into him. An absurd superstition! Young women—you must have noticed—cannot go anywhere without their water bottles. It's the fashion, like a Gucci bag. Even better if the water comes from halfway around the world; very special water they have over there in Fiji, not at all like our own. Ridiculous—100 percent bosh and superstition. If it were only a fashion, well, it would be only a fashion. When physicians and nurses get in on the act, tell lies, and invent nonexistent benefits, it becomes a problem. Superstitions that rule us are a problem.

The list is long. In some parts of the world, homeopathy is an article of faith. To the extent that you can be healed by that in which you believe, the placebo effect, there is nothing against homeopathy. There is also *nothing* for it in the known science of the world. *Nothing.* But this superstition has been around a very long time, and it will be around for a long time to come. One even finds physicians in modern countries who prescribe homeopathic treatments. If they do it knowing that all they seek is a placebo effect, there is nothing to reproach. The fear is that they believe there is more to it. But it's an old commonplace that physicians are for the most part poor scientists.

The difficulty—and I freely grant it—in our modern world is the overdose of information instantly available to us with one click on Google. We have somehow transferred the former notion that "if it is in print, it must be true" to the Internet. Thus we do not easily distinguish—it isn't easy—between truth and falsehood. Opinions are given increasingly stridently, accusations are made, weapons are leveled, and BANG! Let the one who made the most noise win. If we search Google for homeopathy, we'll find every manner of opinion under the sun, pro, con, and confused. We'll find affirmations—attestations, even—that homeopathy cured a case of pancreatic cancer, and we'll find declarations flatly stating that homeopathy has no scientific basis. Because science is always unsettled, we cannot say that homeopathy will never show a benefit. We can, on the other hand, say that as of this writing, homeopathy has no basis in observed science. We must be open in science to all possibilities, openness being the essence of science, but we mustn't allow that perspective to disturb scientific discipline: science is largely based on observation and measurement. If neither of these incline to a conclusion, the premise must be suspect.

So what else? The list is long!

Vitamins? Nonsense! Unless one has a confirmed vitamin deficiency—which is rare—the taking of vitamins is useless, and the taking of megadoses is either useless or potentially harmful. This information has been broadly publicized over the last years, but we ought not to be surprised to learn that it has not dented vitamin sales. People believe. Superstition.

Genetically modified foods: Europe is in an absolute frenzy about them. One would think they had arrived aboard a suspect spaceship from an alien and hostile planet. Instead, if one looks to the science rather than to the mob for instruction, one makes a discovery that is nothing short of a miracle: foods that resist blights and diseases; that multiply yields, feeding the world's poor; and that offer the promise of reduced use of chemicals in agriculture. Americans seem broadly accepting of GM food—Asians, too—but Europeans are positively rabid in their fear … or is it just a commercial ploy to exclude imported foods? Superstition or cynicism?

"Fair-traded goods" is a misnomer if ever there was one. The notion of fair trade is popular with our urban chattering classes: it makes them feel good about themselves … while starving the world's poorest peoples. Oh, sorry! I wasn't supposed to say that. It just ruins a Sunday evening over chardonnay and cheese in the penthouse. Unfortunately, it's true. Fair trade is bosh. Most people who endorse it cannot say what it is, only that it is good. Well, it isn't. It's a mechanism invented by urban rich kids with no knowledge of the world to ensure that "peasants" (an existential concept they read about in their gilded classrooms and occasionally fleetingly visit on green holidays) receive a minimum fair wage. The real-world result is that we buy only from well-off—relatively speaking—small farmers and agricultural laborers while closing our markets to the poorest of the poor, who cannot yet attain our ivory tower minimum fair wage. This is a problem of economics, the same one that makes silly dreamers imagine that by raising the minimum wage, we increase the living standards of the lowest paid among us … whereas in the real world what happens is that we put them out of work. Bravo, rich kids! It is so fine to feel good about oneself.

If we want to help the poor—really help them—we'll kill the asinine and immoral agricultural subsidies which deny the world's poor the markets and the livelihood by which to pull themselves out of poverty. Now, try to begin a discussion about it within the G8. Ronald Reagan, who did try, said afterward that the other world leaders went away so fast he thought he'd broken wind. Better to laugh than to cry. Fair trade? Bosh—in fact, immoral bosh! Another superstition.

Swine flu: to have read the papers and listened to the box, we might have thought it was time to make peace with our maker. Goodness knows how many scare stories assaulted us, each citing a new and as yet unimagined danger from self-appointed experts—in fact, professional chatterers. Anyone who read between the lines—one has to nowadays as, in our infotainment world, pap passes for press—learned that very few people were dying, in fact fewer than from seasonal flu, and for most people symptoms were very mild. What if this had been the news instead of all that terrifying stuff spouted by pseudoscientific pontiffs of pooh? A generation ago, Walter Cronkite would have presented the whole thing with aplomb, emphasizing the mildness of the disease and stressing reassurance based on the best available science. Instead of some self-important surgeon general or director of the Center for Disease Control intoning all of the unknowns surrounding the disease and the implied risks, responsible spokesmen would have cited the low severity of most cases—the fact that in the majority of instances, without a laboratory test, the swine flu was indistinguishable from a common cold.

Instead, the world went mad, recalling the masked terror of the avian flu of some years before. No doubt, there are some nasty viruses abroad in the world, and someday, some nasty virus is going to successfully invade the human population. Shouldn't we reserve our terror—just so we have some left—for when that actually happens? Might we not be better served keeping the cry of wolf for a real, live wolf? Or is life now like choosing the Saturday matinee, seeking out the next and scariest horror film we can find? When even those in traditional positions of responsibility lose their wits, what can we think of our society? Superstition reigns. We are living in a *National Enquirer* world.

Organic food: it's better for you, isn't it? Uh, no, not really. It is more expensive. Some people think it tastes better. It probably does, in some cases, although "organic" is as much a marketing label as an agricultural reality. And here's the clever twist: many people—never to be disabused by their supermarket—think it is somehow "better for nature." Oh, okay, how? The truth is that organic food is in the best of cases tastier, more commonly only a borderline scam, and in the worst of cases a fraud. The Swiss government recently (in September 2009) released a study comparing organic food with standard supermarket foodstuffs, seeking to evaluate nutrition, contamination, and quality. Result? No difference, although in a few cases, the standard supermarket stuff had some lower germ counts. Conclusion, as given by the government minister responsible? Organic food is more expensive, but without benefit to the consumer. It won't change the view of a gaggle of people who have faith in organic food. No harm, really, except that it's part of a vast tide on nonsense about what is natural and what isn't. Superstition.

Windmills: ah, yes, Don Quixote. We are littering the countryside with these darned things, every one of them a golden egg laid by a government subsidy, and incapable of producing an uninterrupted flow of energy or of producing energy at anywhere near a competitive cost. The golden egg is a gift from us, the taxpayer, to clever investors who install windmills because their hearts are in their wallets, not—as they tell us—in doing the right thing. How we remember T. Boone Pickens—no stupid boy he—lecturing us about how he was going to "devote his entire fortune to doing the right thing for the planet" and install a gazillion windmills across the wastelands of Texas. Only he didn't. After much fa-la-la, what happened? What he said happened was some bullroar about the infrastructure not being ready to carry his clean power to the grid. What really happened is that the subsidies he had imagined didn't ultimately add up to the profit he'd anticipated. No one makes money on power from windmills. The money is entirely in the subsidies. After new technologies delivered by the free market bring us yet more abundant and cheaper power than ever before, we'll be left with vast scrap yards of junk across the landscape. Subsidies and superstition: there's a potent combination!

Regarding windmills, it's worth noting that some future technologies may make them cost-effective and capable of supplying uninterrupted power. There recently appeared a Canadian proposal for an airborne windmill, floating at an altitude where wind flow is more reliable, and tethered to the ground. Interesting. Windmills face two problems: the ability in some reasonable number to produce a meaningful amount of power, and the fact that in all cases, we must build and maintain standby generating capacity for 100 percent of the power. The wind just doesn't blow all of the time. Second, there is no viable mechanism for the storage of electrical power. No wind, no power. Windmills are, for now, a great boondoggle making some opportunistic investors very rich. Don't blame them. Blame us. We elected the reprobates who throw our money away.

Y2K: that was a howler! Planes crashing. The power grid collapsing. The entire Internet on the fritz. Toasters not toasting. Everything and anything. The press was worried. Businesses became worried. Financial markets readied themselves for a Wellesian *War of the Worlds* remake. The government secured our arsenal. And nothing happened. Surprised? Serious people weren't. But they weren't consulted. It is so much more fun to frighten oneself silly with impending disaster. Do you remember how the world held its breath? But why? Because a rumor gained circulation and credence in a world far too credulous of any fantastic fear. A generation earlier, the rumormongers would have been laughed out of town. But not now. We've become fey; we are the new Gauls, waiting for the sky to fall upon our heads, perhaps fearing to have angered the gods. What is it with us? Superstition.

Extreme environmentalism: one of the greatest frauds of all time, an astonishing lie that has suborned a not-insignificant part of our scientific community, subverted public policy to the will of a small group of howling prophets of doom in search of salvation, and knocked the peoples of many nations silly. This is a faith-based superstition replacing a missing spirituality in secular societies, entirely without regard for science and scientific process. The subject is so vital, the breadth of the deception so great, that we shall devote a chapter to it. But, be assured: superstition.

Pedophiles working in every day care: rubbish! No doubt, it has happened. And—yes—it must be harshly punished. It's a despicable crime. But that doesn't mean we need to have a witch hunt. Our psychological police discovered that if properly worked over, small children can be made to say pretty much anything. Obviously we're dealing with a generation that did not grow up with Art Linkletter. So we had three-year-olds using medical terms that would confound most high-school graduates, describing in clinical detail how Mr. So-and-So had "touched me there." Really? Where did they get the astonishing vocabulary? It took a bit of coaching, that.

In the United Kingdom the suspicion of pedophiles lurking behind—no, in front of!—every shrub has grown to a fever. Now parents will no longer be allowed to supervise their *own* children at public playgrounds unless they have been vetted by a criminal investigation. This is not a joke. Are we entirely mad? Who puts this rubbish forth?

In fact, speaking of the United Kingdom, we can gratify all of our lunatic needs just by reading the London daily press. There is nothing sufficiently absurd for today's London editors. They will print anything, and do so every day. It's a frenzy to see who can be the most hysterical, who can conjure the next greatest disaster. If it were all tabloid entertainment, it wouldn't actually matter, but it is not; now it is the mainstream papers, those that used to be known as the serious press, who vie with each other for sensational stories of no respectable provenance. The *Times* employs an editor, Benjamin Webster, who will exaggerate anything fed to him by his co-religionists in the extreme environmental movement, with no regard whatsoever for truth. His Murdoch bosses look the other way. If the story sells, it's good enough. Stashes of cash and an army of lawyers protect them just as the mob in New York protects itself. The mystery is why people who are apparently literate still buy all this bosh.

What is it with us that makes us so credulous, so willingly gulled? Do we no longer pay attention? Do we no longer count the failed predictions? In 1974 the world suffered a petroleum crisis through the economic unwisdom of certain powerful governments, the United States first among them. A herd of experts—who were anything but—surfaced to predict in the gravest stentorian tones that we had been wicked and for our sins we would run out of petroleum by 1980, then 1984, then 1992, and finally 1996. Oh. Now it's 2009 and our proven reserves are greater than they have ever been. The running out has been postponed. Oh. Yet, we saw it on charts and we heard it from computer models that there just wasn't any more petroleum left, that nature's revenge was at hand, that we were to be condemned to a cold and dark existence for having driven our lusty V-8s. More recently—amid the Katrina nonsense—that bloviating blowhard Al Gore informed us that we were going to suffer more and greater storms—biblical storms, no doubt—than ever before because we had again been wicked, this time tampering with carbon dioxide. Experts at all sorts of green-cause institutes were wheeled in to say amen and did so on cue. Nature failed to cooperate or wasn't told, and the years following mischievously refused to deliver. The only wind left was Gore's. How is it we're blown around by this stuff?

The unsettling thing is that the inmates have taken over the asylum, such that now organizations that ought to be reliable and credible are not. This is how the National Hurricane Center delivers itself of predictions that utterly fail—every time—and still maintains public credibility. Various expert weather analysts weigh in with curiously similar—shall we say suspiciously similar?—predictions … and fall flat on their faces. Yet we listen. Why? Why? Why?

Allergies: know anyone who does not have an allergy? Where did we suddenly get all these allergies? Too many allergy docs, methinks. Look, 90 percent of us don't have any sort of condition that qualifies as a proper allergy. And maybe 1 percent of us can have some sort of real allergic reaction to something. Yes, I know, pollen in the air gives us a bit of a sniffle, an occasional sneeze. Buy some Kleenex. The treatment of small irritations under the guise of allergy medicine is quackery. An allergy is something physically serious. My mother had a friend who was allergic to dog hair—really allergic. She couldn't breathe, her face would redden alarmingly, and her autonomic nervous system would short-circuit. That's an allergy. Now these pestilential allergy docs diagnose every kid who walks in the door with an allergy, and their soccer moms believe it. Unbelievable! No common sense at all. Only superstition.

Sects and cults: we are awash in off-the-wall sects and cults, each one professing to have seen the light. To be honest, there always were these eddies in the mainstream of faith, but they rarely attracted more than small notice and some derision. I mean no offense. Religion needs to be like meatloaf, filling and consistent. It gives us pause, leads us to reflection, offers solace, and is there when we need it. It oughtn't to drive us out of doors in the night to howl at the moon. When, as a society, we see the mainstream—meatloaf—faiths fracture and break into smaller and smaller bits, something is wrong. A man can believe in his own way without having to break with his church, so to speak. A breach ought to be reserved for fundamental differences, not for nuances.

I haven't a thing against each one of us meeting God—or not meeting him at all—in our own way. That's freedom of conscience, the liberty to be who I am. But is it really necessary to caterwaul about the land and to be a pest about it? And what does it say when we do? My guess would be that it speaks of an unsettled soul, an unease, a quest, a need, a query. Surely the answer—believer or unbeliever—ought never to be superstition. Faith in God fills the entire void, leaving no room for strange or evil spirits; it is light itself. Secular certainty, by definition, excludes spirits: everything is natural, mechanical, and ordered. In either case, superstition has no place. Yet our world seems replete with superstition. Perhaps we have found ourselves unable to cleave to the God of our fathers, yet no more able to believe in nothing. The solution has been, it seems, the worst of both of these worlds: a primitive superstition, a belief in every odd spirit that courses our senses, a desperate latching on to shards of broken-glass intuitions promoted as truth ... strange life buoys indeed.

Disaster movies: these may say it all. We are in a time when to believe in disasters and catastrophes seems more normal than not. We have a dark need to suffer, to be made to suffer, to expiate our souls. May I recommend the Church of Rome? It grants absolution. Tried and true, simpler and healthier. It is not my purpose to promote any church, but to speak of mainstream churches. By and large, a good variety of these abounds, at least as many as there are cakes in a pastry shop on a Tuesday morning, and they seem to have done yeoman duty by generations of penitents. I recommend that we go back to them. They're not perfect, subject as they are to all the vagaries and jealousies and hypocrisies of man. But they have stood the test of time, they have shed cults into oblivion, and they offer a durable litany. When I speak of church, I speak generically: temple, mosque, meetinghouse, whatever, but for goodness' sake, something straightforward and mainstream. Back to the disaster movies: of course there is a pleasure in a simple thrill; it is the essence of the thriller. In some way, we have always taken enjoyment from fright, but not real fright—make-believe fright. Campfire tales. Ghost stories. Murders on stormy, foggy nights.

The disturbing thing before us now is the blurring—association?—of true fright with some sort of entertainment, a continuation of the Cinema 3 horror movie in the parking lot. We need to keep the disaster movies inside the cinemaplex. We need to understand that they are fiction. I give you for example the celebrated film *An Inconvenient Truth*, which, given the number of serious errors it contains can only be considered a work of fiction. Where is the line? How do we distinguish anymore between the weekend's new disaster movie, Mr. Gore's production, and a very real earthquake ... that we see only on TV? Our judgment, our critical eye, needs a splash of cold water.

Superstition is a threat to our tranquility and good judgment for it substitutes the fantastic for the real and confounds us. Some it renders apoplectic. A hallmark of sanity, at least of equanimity, of adulthood, is the separation of fact from fiction.

Superstition is fiction.

Chapter 5
Tilting at Windmills

The world needs to be run by grown-ups. Not easy to find anymore, a grown-up. There was a time when adult males knew what to do at the scene of an accident. Adult females also knew, but the rule was they only displayed this knowledge when there weren't any adult males around. Now these tough guys stand about wringing their hands and shaking like the leaves of a Hitchcock autumn, waiting for "emergency personnel" to arrive. When these self-important uniforms finally do arrive, their priority is to assert authority. "Stand back!" they order the crowd of three. If any one of three doesn't step back smartly, he'll get a proper dressing-down. It reminds me of the story—similar circumstances—of a doctor who had been first at the scene. The emergency personnel arrived and of course pushed him aside, leaving him to tell them, "When you get to the part about calling the doctor, he's here." In my state, we have increased the number of troopers in our state police over 51 percent in a time during which our population increased 18 percent. Was there a problem before? Not that anyone knew. How do we employ these puffed-up cowboys? Well, I'll tell you how. We no longer allow—by law—a construction worker to be flagman and traffic controller on his own responsibility at a construction site. We post a trooper there at huge expense, to watch him. Have we gotten any benefit from this? Uh, no. Why do we do it? Because the state police mau-maued the legislature into a law designed to provide them with cushy work. What did they do to achieve this? Easy. They got some friendly experts to testify that this would make the site safe. Really? Officers sitting in their cars, yakking on their cell phones, or standing around gawking at an excavator like a truant boy? Citizens have even been cowed into buying the silly "Troopers are our best protection" stickers and plastering them on their cars.

In Chapter 1, I already described how the state has overwhelmed any vestige of democracy with money and numbers: our money, buying us. I have used the example of the troopers at highway construction sites—a scandal in many states—as an example. One cannot find a motorist who doesn't understand the game. But we don't do anything about it. If we try—and I dare you to do it—the troopers will beat the tom-toms and gather their legions of allies about them: firemen, emergency medical personnel, teachers, soccer moms, and silly, toothless old boys—"good citizens"—fearful of their very shades. You will be scorned by all these self-anointed good citizens and pronounced an ogre, a crackpot, a scrooge, and likely a lot worse. No one will speak up for you, even though the majority knows you are right.

What we have is a failed democracy in which we have ceded the field to a gang of muggers who have stolen "freedom" for themselves and made it into a mockery that has nothing to do with liberty. The very meaning of the word "liberty" has been twisted and perverted. They are God's own "freedom army," and woe to anyone who suggests otherwise. In my state the governor and the legislature are obedient; they will never cross this army. The problem is people telling each other what is not true, because it's the accepted thing to do. I recall an incisive description of political correctness as "A manner of comportment and speech that is publicly represented but privately meaningless." Exactly!

Thus do we come to windmills—the real ones and those of Don Quixote's imagination. We have already spoken of the physical ones, those comprising the global scam that makes the naive feel good about themselves and that does precisely nothing for the environment, arguably the contrary, as we litter untold numbers of pretty ridges with this erector-set junk. There is solace in knowing that most of them will rust and decompose in a few hundred years. At least they aren't forever. With any luck, the ones at sea will sink. Maybe they'll make good reefs for fish. We seem to place the mom rule of "doing something" ahead of the dad rule, which used to be "make sure it works."

Any cursory study of history will lead us to understand that man has always lied to himself through rumor, myth, superstition, and falsehood. You can't fix that. However, there have been periods wherein veracity was treated with greater respect and periods wherein it wasn't. When veracity was the flavor of the day, we tended to be in periods of relative enlightenment, away from the superstition of which I have spoken. From today's news we learn the following:

Item: Jellyfish are "invading" (must be bad) northern waters, because of—Yes! You guessed it, but no prize; it was all too obvious—climate change!

- Item: Hawaiian beaches are showing accelerated erosion, because of—oh, no fair, you already know.
- This represents *one day's* news. Each day it's the same, the unrelenting drumbeat of hooey. Does the originator of the jellyfish story have any understanding at all of life on earth, of animal and fish and insect populations? They are *ever* changing and *ever* variable. They have *never* been stable. Get it? This is at the level of what used to be high-school science. Now, of course, high schools don't do science anymore; they do social consciousness, which is no more than the myth of the day. As for the silliness regarding the Hawaiian beaches, let us direct its originator to any Geology 101 textbook. Erosion is one of the principle geological mechanisms. That's how the Grand Canyon was cut. Now there is a truly scary global warming story: huge gash opens in Earth! Wow! Day after day after day, we are served up this hash without the least critical inquiry. It's a problem. It's a big problem.
- The world—sorry for this—does *not* believe in "global warming." It is only an impression we have in the wealthy Western social democracies. In a sense it's a rich man's disease, like gout, but

much more invidious. We will inquire into the why of this disease, but for now we need to recognize that

(a) Two of the world's largest nations, China and India, and the world's second military power, Russia, do not believe in global warming. (If we keep our eye on the ball, we'll notice that they duck out of any commitment regarding climate change, but artfully feign concern. This is to please us, as a follower of one faith may stand respectfully by as the follower of another goes through his ablutions and prayers; it doesn't signify conversion.);

(b) The world's poorest nations—which, contrary to the perspective that obtains in the capitals of the Western social democracies—can read, and more to the point count, are all for global warming. Have we noticed how many billions—trillions—it is under discussion to give them as "reparations" for the damage prosperous nations have done? It doesn't take the imagination of a Twain to figure out what is going on here. It's money. Watch the not-so-poor join the queue. It'll be a game of pin the donkey on the tail. Who wouldn't join the bread line?

(c) This leaves the "polite anomalies," such as Japan, who do not want to offend their, ahem, customers. They smile, they bow, they move their lips, and they don't mean a word of it.

We can put two interpretations on this: either all of these countries are truly devoid of any scientific understanding and utterly contemptuous of their own futures … or they actually understand all too well that the wealthy Western nations have gotten their knickers in a twist, and they will just stand by until the fever abates. As in so many other matters concerning human behavior, watch not what they say, but what they do. Putin was his usual clever self, declaring that Russia would do her part, but … ah! … proper "carbon credit" will have to be given to Russia's vast Siberian forests, such that—in effect—Russia's part will be … uh … nothing. Well done, Vlad! And all the Western emperors nodded their heads in appreciation. The reason Russia will do nothing—pay attention now—is that the Russian Academy of Sciences doesn't agree that the evidence supports global warming. It is not possible—please, God—that all of our Western leaders are really so stupid. No, there's something else going on. It's about power and control and money, which is what tyranny has always been about. Tony Blair's Alfred E. Neumannesque face pops up. As Virgil wrote, *"agnosco veterem flammam."* It wasn't the same context, but close enough.

One thing leads to another, and so windmills take us to nuclear power plants. Let's have it out: the propeller heads caused us to miss the boat on nuclear power, caused untold amounts of real pollution—and also CO_2—by their clamor, retarded the evolution of nuclear technology, which is the future, and made a great many petroleum producers very rich. Now, do we put the propeller heads at the head of the class, or in the corner with a dunce cap? While our green advocates were browning our country, France became the world leader in peaceful nuclear technology and now generates over 80 percent of her power cleanly, safely, and economically. What happened to the rest of us is what happens when the grown-ups leave the room and the children escape the playpen; things get broken. The quest for clean, abundant, and efficient energy was irresponsibly postponed by thirty years. Compared to France and Japan, we're in the dark ages of energy, now fussing with children's toys—windmills, woodstoves, and widgets—while the grown-ups run their high-tech energy grids. A few of our 1960s and 1970s environmentalists—the ones we have to thank for our antiquated and dirty energy infrastructure—have at least come forward and confessed their sins. They have admitted that they were wrong. It's a decent enough step at the personal level, but it hardly remedies the problem. Now the next generation of idlers, dreamers, and activists are up to the next generation of tricks. They've already been responsible for another major boner and environmental disaster, the ethanol scam. What will be their next belly flop?

What happened to nuclear power in the United States that did not happen in France and Japan? There probably isn't a single explanation. The fact that in the 1960s we had oil and gas and coal is most assuredly a part of it, but what really stopped our nuclear energy dead was superstition. We just weren't going to trust the newfangled technology, casting our lot with those who at the end of the nineteenth century weren't going to have electricity in their homes. Well, I have a proposal for the twenty-first century: from now on, those who superstitiously obstruct new energy technologies shall have their power cut off.

The French are culturally superstitious but not technologically so. Maybe their schools just do a better job of giving the average student a reasonable grounding in basic science, so the fission of atoms for the production of energy is a comprehensible physical process, not the frightening black magic so many Americans take it to be. There is other evidence for this point of view. At least twenty years after France had proven the utility and reliability of a nationwide high-speed rail network, a network that has not had a single accident to date—a network powered by clean nuclear power—the governors of the New England states gathered with the purpose of "inquiring into the feasibility of high-speed rail travel." Nobody laughed. Japan had the bullet train, France had the TGV—both swift, efficient, and massively popular—and there we were asking ourselves, *Mais est-ce possible?* The real question is the mathematical possibility of having five governors in the same place at the same time whose joined IQs leaves the advantage to the temperature on a January day.

The French found another benefit in their nuclear infrastructure: heat. Since the demand for power drops considerably during the graveyard shift, and since nuclear plants operate best at steady output, the energy industry offered electricity at deep discounts in the depth of the night, allowing concrete floors in industrial and commercial spaces to be warmed. These floors act as heat sinks and give good warmth the rest of the day, long after the power has been turned off. Clever, *n'est ce pas?* We missed that boat too.

California—the state we most rely upon for aberrant notions—legislated some sort of phantasmagorical mandate regarding electric cars. Pot is more or less legal in California—not a bad thing—but the legislators ought to forbear during business hours. Next they will legislate how the rain must fall. Anyway, they in their collective wisdom, ignoring the battery technology of the day, mandated that something like 10 percent of cars sold in California had to be electric by a given date, and never mind that California had so managed its power rates as to ensure critical shortages of electricity. In the interim, entirely beyond the scope or ken of the legislature, technology brought us hybrids, a far more elegant and practical solution for the promotion of fuel economy. This is the eternal problem with legislation. It is always, as the French expression has it, *avec un train de retard* (one train behind). So, we want to impose a solution that isn't one while the free market's ingenuity brings us a very good one.

The Japanese government's MITI was established for the promotion of modern technologies and has had the usual success of government initiatives in this regard, having taken a great deal of good money from Japanese taxpayers and thrown it at bad projects. MITI has an almost perfect record of failure. The free market did one end run after another on the "solutions" MITI promoted. The problem with government is that it is not good at changing course. Our modern world changes course every day—in fact, every hour of every day. This isn't a proclamation or even a suggestion of the saintliness of the private sector—even if it has brought more good to more people than any social organization in the history of man—but rather an affirmation of the creativity of the individual left unfettered to pursue his own happiness, ideas, hopes, and profit. The logic is irrefutable: a hundred million people motivated by their individual gain will outperform a million government drones by many orders of magnitude. That is what the collectivists never understand, the unique and irrepressible force of the individual. We'll pursue our theme, but first—can't wait on this one—a fresh howler from today's news.

Listen to this: "Condoms Can Reduce Global Warming." No kidding! That was the headline. It's a joke, right? No, sorry, it isn't. Wish it were. But, it needs to be treated as one. So, ready? Here's how it goes. People—bad, bad people—are the cause of Global Warming, capital G, capital W. So, if we have less people—that's where the condoms come in—we'll have less GW! Clever, isn't it? But why stop there? We could borrow the Lenin-Stalin-Mao gambit and just shoot millions of people. Did I say millions? I meant hundreds of millions. Now, that would reduce GW for sure! Better yet we could shoot those who can read and write first, as surely they are the mischief makers, designing and building all those bad, bad factories and using doomsday technologies like toasters and lawn mowers. But wait, it gets better yet. If we get rid of half of humanity, we can slaughter a bunch of flatulent cows and slay the methane dragon—a greenhouse gas many times worse than CO^2 according to the Extreme Green Litany. Once we have dispensed with those who can read and write, and the cows they keep for milk and meat—for the readers and writers are also evil meat-eaters—we can revert to a simpler, natural life, where those who remain die off from disease and starvation, no longer equipped with the modern skills to forestall these. It just keeps getting better! And then—now it's so good I'm breathless—comes the ultimate, a plague of locusts that strips the planet bare and then itself dies as the last vegetable matter is consumed. After a small period of cannibalism as the insects eat each other, it will all be over. No life will remain, no GW anymore, and the planet can revert to one of its regular guises from geologic time: an ice ball. What a triumph! It's as one of those games of Chinese checkers where you finally figure out a way to eliminate even the last marble!

I have another solution. All prospective parents shall be subjected to genetic typing, and if their combined genes carry any risk of producing a future green lunatic, they shall be required to use condoms throughout their reproductive lives, *every time*. Actually that solves two problems at one go.

As we have come to the very large reservoir—inexhaustible I should think—of stupidity, I take the occasion to direct your attention to a Swiss environmental movement, protesting outside fancy restaurants because … because … because they serve, yes, frogs' legs. What, you ask, is the rationale? It is cruel to kill frogs to eat their legs. Ah. If I am not mistaken, we kill steers to eat their flanks, no? And we kill chickens to eat their breasts and thighs and legs, no? And we kill lobsters to eat their tails and claws, no? So, how did a frog come to be so sainted? Let us guess. A frog is green? A frog lives in a pond that is a wetland? A frog is cute, as in Kermit? One of the Swiss greenies has a frog as a pet? A sister who looks like a frog? I give up. I don't know. I don't care.

It's just too stupid. This is what we deal with in the rich-kid modern world, run by children who ought to be beyond their formative years and who have far too much time on their hands and far too little matter in their heads, casting about—because Papa and Mama made life too easy for them—for something meaningful to do. Try getting a job and supporting yourself. Stop being a parasite. See if you can do something productive. How is that for meaningful?

It is not my wish to provide a catalogue of inanity. Examples are rife. I do no more than cite a grab bag of instances. Any one of us can add an essentially endless number of samples. Nor is it my wish to emphasize the obvious, that there are some terribly foolish things in the world. That would be banal, having been true in Assyria, Alexandria, Athens, Rome, Byzantium, Samarkand, Samarang, and Sausalito. What is different now, as it has been cyclically in the history of man, is the attention given the foolishness. That is a problem. We in the West are given, at this juncture in time, to a credulousness that defies any modern perspective, and we see this broadly in all things. We have touched on sufficient illustrative examples, suggesting a host of others that any reader can readily add, such that the point is in effect demonstrated. QED. That has been my purpose, to *prove* a case, to demonstrate beyond reasonable doubt that we do in fact face a problem. It isn't clear what we can do about it.

Chapter 6
The '89 Château Haut-Brion Wager

It is a damned fine bottle of wine, the '89 Haut-Brion. The wager is simple: First, that within three years—that would be by January 1, 2013—the CO^2 theory of global warming will be largely discredited; second, that by the same date the anthropogenic cause of climate change will be widely disbelieved; and third, that this shall be judged by a mutually agreed upon neutral body. Now, it's true that the '89 Haut-Brion isn't cheap. But if, as those pressing global warming upon us so vigorously tell us, it's all true and more than true, there shouldn't be any risk. I have yet to find a taker. Many to whom I proposed the wager responded with anger. You can make of it what you want. I have my opinion.

Global warming, understood as the notion that man has caused a severe and destabilizing climate change that would not have occurred absent man, is the greatest scientific fraud since the Ptolemaic universe. It is a monumental falsehood predicated upon no science at all, supported by a body of people whose purpose is political, and vetted by a group of scientists who are—in coarse prison vernacular—their bitches. I gather that makes me "a denier," that silly label invented by the social revolutionaries behind the GW movement to denigrate any opinion contrary to their own. In Soviet times, recalcitrant souls were branded saboteurs and shot. It is always the same with these once-more-recycled revolutionaries: play their game, or die. In my state, "Live free or die" is our state motto. I think I'll live free.

The GW movement has swept up naive conservationists, cynical or just stupid politicians, a great gallery of those in the media, and—with some hesitation, it's true—a large number of people across the Western world who, against all experience, believe the celebrity classes, the opinion leaders, and worst of all, their politicians. Al Gore is an easy target; he is such a palpable buffoon. Here is a man who has spent his life in luxury, consuming ten times the energy of an average citizen; living in a house that would do a small hotel proud; driving vehicles that are more nearly trucks than cars; and flying here and there on his mission of self-promotion in private planes. Now, he wants us to believe in his commitment to the environment. We ought to run the scoundrel out of town on a rail, if we could find one to support him! Actually, Al Gore is such an easy target that we will largely pass him by—no skill to it.

Far more despicable are the alchemists of GW, those scientists who have sold their souls for gold. It is not credible that these, in their majority, have been so beguiled by the GW mantra that they have forgotten, or set aside, all of their scientific training. Of course, one thing we must note is that when we deal with groups like the Union of Concerned Scientists—sounds impressive, doesn't it?—we in fact deal with a group wherein only very few have climate-relevant credentials. Thus we get an impression of the thing that isn't true simply from all those doctoral degrees they flash in front of us. But, need I really point out that a PhD in psychology doesn't cut it for climate expertise? Moreover, you get those who have been bamboozled. For example, ask one thousand geophysicists—any thousand you care to choose—if there is "climate change," and you will inevitably get one thousand "aye"s, unless one of the congregation is asleep in the back. Why? Because any geophysicist will tell you that there is always climate change, always has been, and always will be, so far as we can tell. So when you misuse honest scientific judgments to support a political cause you can get pretty much the outcome you want.

It is the same, in fact, with the vaunted computer models of the GW crowd. In the early days of data processing—of the digital age—programmers soon found the acronym GIGO to describe an inevitable weakness of computers: garbage in, garbage out.

Weather can be reliably forecasted in the earth's temperate zones for little more than twenty-four hours, sometimes less. The forty-eight-hour forecast is more reliable than not. The seventy-two-hour forecast becomes questionable but is still of some utility, and beyond that, it's the guessing zone. The reason is that the factors influencing weather are of enormous complexity and subject to interactions we do not even now fully understand. I do not believe that I need to further press this argument. Most of us know this to be true by our common experience of rainy picnics.

Some of us, the skiers or beachgoers, for example, please ourselves by seeing that a seasonal forecast favors our indulgence. "The winter will be colder and snowier than normal" makes winter sports fans smile. However, any among them who is older than twelve already knows that this sort of seasonal forecast is prone to error—regularly and fatally so. It wasn't forty-five days ago—as I write—that all the reliable weather experts predicted a warmer and dryer than normal winter for the American Northwest and the Canadian Southwest. It hasn't stopped snowing since, relentlessly, in the heaviest early season snowfalls in memory. The fact is that short of major and well-known weather patterns such as El Niño, long-range weather forecasting is almost 100 percent unreliable. Weather is not climate, but if we can't untangle the complexities of weather, what makes us suppose that we've got climate right?

Is there in fact any reason to suppose that climate forecasts are reliable? In the years between 1976 and 1998, a measurable small warming of the planet occurred. Let us set aside for a moment whether this was a part of a natural cycle or a result of anthropogenic causes. The GW crowd's computer models had a field day! Dante's hell was only a fantasy of the poet's imagination. The omnipotent computer models showed us a real hell, one that would truly and sternly punish us for our sins. We saw curves showing the relentless progression of the sweltering heat and the dying off of crickets, chipmunks, buffalo, and probably our brothers-in-law, and these were now "beyond doubt"—anyone calling them into question, or even asking a question, was just a reprobate, an evil "denier."

But a funny thing happened. Nature hadn't been informed, and in 1998 the warming stopped. At first it wasn't anything to worry about, just a little glitch, but as the years passed, it became embarrassing. The response from the GW temple was predictable: strike the Big Lie Gong frantically and loudly and indict those who hear through the noise as heretics. Indeed, do not stop at that. Gather the kindling and ready the auto-da-fé. To the stake with them! But again a massively contrary Mother Nature stuck her tongue out. The decade passed, and the temperature simply refused to resume its upward course. It became a serious matter, but never fear: a computer model that has been programmed to show one thing can be reprogrammed to show another. And so it was that "adjustments" were made, and mirabile dictu, the "corrected" model showed—surprise!—that the intense warming of the GW model would have "cooling periods," after which the warming would return with a vengeance. Neat, huh? Yes. Much too neat, in fact.

A word more on the label "denier." From a propaganda standpoint, it was a fine choice, full of negative connotation, with a suggestion of crackpot-ism and a soupçon of evil. The subject demands something better than name-calling. We are speaking of something that, if true, could have important consequences, and no less important ones if untrue. The "better safe just in case" argument doesn't cut it. One doesn't jump into a maelstrom because someone might be within needing rescue; one needs to be rather sure.

The hypothesis is, rendered to its bones, this: man's existence—and more to the point, industrial activity—have unbalanced nature, the natural equilibrium of our atmosphere, with the result that we have provoked an unnatural change in the climate that menaces us all. This is false.

- There is *no* constant natural equilibrium on our planet, and there never has been;

- Through geologic time the planet has been (a) much warmer, (b) much colder, (c) entirely free of any ice, actually about 80 percent of the time, (d) entirely covered by ice, a small percentage of the time, and (e) more or less temperate with ice at the poles and at altitude, some of the time.

- There is no "tipping point." The geologic evidence is clear. Indeed, the CO^2 theory of GW cannot be deduced from anything in the geologic record. The concentration of CO^2 in the atmosphere has been less than today and orders of magnitude greater than that of today, yet the planet curiously "recovered" (i.e., changed) in complex cycles, 99.9 percent of which occurred not only before the industrial age, but indeed before man walked the earth. The notion of irreversible anything on our planet is entirely without scientific basis. It is science fiction, made to scare the kiddies. Whether the purpose is for the kiddies to frighten themselves or others can be argued, but what is unarguable is the falsity of the affirmation.

- Any investigation of GW *must* begin with a study of our planet's history, which can be read for a nanosecond during the time of man's history but otherwise is recorded only in the geologic record. That which has occurred in man's time, the nanosecond, is about as good an indicator of events as a snapshot taken of a ball two inches away from a swung bat is an indicator of the outcome of a ball game. It is utterly meaningless. One thousand, ten thousand, or fifty thousand years are of no interpretive value in a continuum of 4.5 billion years. Mathematics are less well understood than they once were—when a high-school diploma meant something—so let's just do the division: 50,000 is 1/90,000 of 4.5 billion. If we equated that to a man's average 76-year life, it would represent 7.4 hours. What can we know of a life from 7.4 hours of it? A little, but not much. Now, let's look at the period our GW fans use: normally less than 100 years of Earth's history, often less than 30 years. This period is used for a basic reason: it is only during the last 30 years that we have

79

somewhat accurately measured the base data. So, what is 30 years of 4.5 billion? 1/150,000,000, which would represent—equated to the 76-year life of which we spoke—16 seconds. What could we know from a 16-second observation of a man's life? And, more to the point, what could we predict?

- Any reliance on a computer model must begin with a well-known given: in a complex system where the data is for practical purposes infinite, it will not be possible to enter anything more than an infinitely small amount of the data into the program. Planetary climate and weather being systems of enormous complexity—for our purposes, infinite even without joining the necessary considerations of crust, core, space, sun, and cosmic phenomena—we will have to pick and choose which data to enter, and there is the entire mischief: the capability of our information technology is dwarfed—overwhelmed is the correct word—by the data it would have to handle to give even a suggestion of fidelity to fact. Our observation period has been so limited as to render the data we have entirely inadequate, and the choice of the data used *compels* the outcome. Critics will say that the procedures were "peer reviewed" (i.e., vetted by independent teams) and I will tell you that this could have been fairly said of decisions handed down by the Inquisition. Even exempting bad faith and lucre (grants), it is the lemming effect. Moreover, the data of which we speak, whose historical accuracy in our own time is suspect—without speaking of any longer period that must necessarily be a hypothesis—(i.e., guess, or in the best of cases "informed guess"), is like all scientific measurement accurate within a plus-minus range. A temperature measured as 16°C is not actually measured—scientifically speaking—as 16°C, but as 16°C +/– 0.3°C, therefore something between 15.7°C and 16.3°C, which matters enormously, even if it is no more than nitpicking in our daily lives: 15.7°C entered in a database may give a cooling trend when extrapolated for a hundred years, 16°C may give a slight warming, and 16.3°C may give a strong warming. So, which was it? 15.7°C, 16°C, or 16.3°C? We don't know. The data collection is subject to this range of error. Which number did the computer modeler use? It *really* matters. Which one did he *choose* and *why*? Now multiply the same effect across one hundred variables.

- Science is *not* based on computer models. Computer models are *games* that can be useful to suggest lines of inquiry, but that have *no value* in predicting the future. If they did, I suggest to you, there would be a large number of very rich geeks who would have broken the code on foreign-exchange-rate movements, a vastly simpler—in fact infinitely simpler—equation than that which represents climate. Science is based on *observation* and *measurement*. What we can observe on our planet is the geologic record. That record tells us beyond reasonable doubt that *variability* is the inherent nature of our planet, and that variability gives us some lovely things and some not very nice ones: plate tectonics, earthquakes, volcanoes, noxious natural gases, floods, droughts, intense cold, searing heat, and *change*. The planet has only one constant: *change*. Now, for extra points, go to your room and sort out what change is natural and what change is man-made. No fair looking at Pamela Anderson.

- Correlation is not causation. Winston Churchill humorously remarked that having studied the matter with care, he could declare that soda water makes you drunk, it being the obvious common element in scotch and soda, gin and soda, and vodka and soda. The GW crowd take a snippet in time, observe that during that snippet temperatures have risen and so has atmospheric CO^2, and deduce that CO^2 is the cause. One might have imagined they would have had the humility—in science, humility really matters—to try to see if (a) the same obtained in previous warmings and (b) which preceded the other. The cause rarely follows the event. What the geologic record shows is that past warming periods were unrelated to spikes—some many times higher than the present one—in atmospheric CO^2. Oh.

- We keep hearing of *atmospheric* CO^2, at least when the speaker bothers to specify it or understands why it's important. This is because the *sea* holds vastly more CO^2 than the atmosphere, and *rocks* hold most of all. Surprised? One interpretation of a relationship—if there is a meaningful one—between CO^2 and temperature is that a warming might trigger an increased release of CO^2 from seawater, a sort of "bubbling" effect. But in that case the warming would be the cause of the CO^2 increase, not the other way around.

- The GW guys attach every type of catastrophe to warming. The carousel of horrors is too well-known to repeat: the floods; the droughts (come on, guys, make up your minds); the famines; the plagues; the *earthquakes* for goodness' sake; and probably your Irish Setter not wanting to chase a stick anymore, just for good measure. Now, once again referring to the geologic record, let's get one thing straight: warmth is much better than cold for life on our planet. Life thrived in warm periods and died back in cold periods. One of the reasons is that cold periods tend to lead to desertification as a cool atmosphere evaporates less water than a warm one, and there is thus less precipitation. As for CO^2, aside from its irrelevance for temperature, it is *not* a pollutant but an inert common gas—as oxygen—vital to life. Plants grow better with higher levels of CO^2, and life is lush. The great die-backs have been in *cold* periods. Even in our recent recorded history we only survived—well, some did anyway—the period known as the Little Ice Age, from roughly 1600 to 1900. Rivers froze far to the south in Europe, crops failed, disease raged, and people died. Life is hard in cold periods.

- Sea levels, the nightmare of Al Gore, were conjured by the simple expedient of having moved the decimal point to the left on his predicted rise. When this story started out, the line was that if the polar ice cap melted, New York would drown. It took quite a while for the kiddies to learn about isostasy: it's easy enough to verify with a glass of water and an ice cube. Anyway, now they get it and they've dropped the subject. So, what does Nobel Laureate Gore know of sea levels? Not much, apparently. If he did, he'd know that sea levels have changed dramatically over the course of geologic time, and he'd also know that there isn't a damned thing we can do about it. I do not know what this savant knows about plate tectonics, but if he wants for excitement, he could read up on that for his next film. Continental drift is really scary. Earthquakes! Volcanoes! Tsunamis! Mountain ranges violently thrusting up! Seas invading continents! Great lakes emptying all of a sudden! Gads, Mabel, that's frightenin' stuff. Don't you be lookin', now. Fact: sea levels have ranged up and down within a 200- meter (660-foot) range, at times adding millions of square miles of dry land to the continents—the continental shelves—and at times submerging entire sections of continents. There ain't nuthin Big Al can do about it. Nature 1, Big Al 0. He's pissing out of his league.

- I like ice, snow, and cold—it's pretty. It's a good thing I'm living now, because for most of our planet's history, there wasn't *any* ice. None. Nowhere. Oh. As pretty as ice is, it isn't fantastic for kitchen gardens, family farms, or vineyards. So—duh—things grow better where there isn't any ice. What is ice good for? Skiing, at least if the ice is in its softer form, snow. Drinks. Tourism. Penguins? All right, seriously now. The world as we know it has ice, with most of the planet's ice locked up in the icecaps. Antarctica is the gorilla. Greenland is pretty substantial in its own right, but paltry next to the southern continent. What we know about ice is this: in geologic time, the presence of ice is definitely limited—about 20 percent of our planet's history—and in man's time ice is extremely variable at its fringes. Fringes? Yes. The Arctic Sea—the polar icecap, therefore, *never* very thick; the coastal ice of Greenland and Antarctica, including sea ice; and the world's valley glaciers are all considered the fringes. Compared to the Greenland and Antarctic icecaps, this fringe ice just doesn't amount to much, less than 10 percent of the total. And it is very variable, even year to year. We don't know why, but as that variability is thoroughly recorded prior to the Industrial Age, we're just going to have to think it's natural. There are many hypotheses: variability of sunlight, sun energy, cosmic rays, cloud cover, deep ocean currents, et cetera. Maybe it's all of them combined. As we have said, the planet's climate is a *very* complex system, for the purpose of our present state of knowledge and technology, an *infinitely* complex system. If you wish to be convinced and reassured regarding the variability of ice, read the logs of the Nantucket and New Bedford whaling fleets of the nineteenth century. You will see that year to year, captains recorded startling changes in sea ice, finding one year that Baffin Bay was open water to Thule, in the northwest of Greenland, and the very next season, closed in a line from Godthab to Frobisher Bay, more than two-thirds of the way south. Let us put some perspective on this: it means a twelve-month change in sea ice of more than 300,000 square kilometers (120,000 square miles), an area the size of California. Oh. This is without speaking of their sometimes finding leads (open water) that allowed them to fish the gulfs, straits, and channels of Canada's arctic islands, an area as large as all of Europe, and at other times to be suddenly frozen in—ice bound—for a season, if they were fortunate, sometimes two … or for eternity with bad luck. The GW folks never speak of this. Embarrassing. Ah, but did I tell you about the polar bears?

• Okay, polar bears. I really love these magnificent predators. My sailboat is named *Nanuq*, Inuit for "polar bear." These creatures are magic: enormous and powerful and solitary, with an intelligence that a man must fear, a sense of smell that will detect a living thing twenty miles away, and a body as well adapted to the sea as to the land. And they're gorgeous. What they are not is cute. A polar bear is an animal whose entire purpose is to kill. What the popular myth does not tell us is that polar bears are very adaptable to warmer and colder temperatures; that, being omnivorous, they will feed on anything, including man; and—note this well, class—that 85 percent of polar bears are in stable or growing populations, and 15 percent are in *one* decreasing population. There are *more* polar bears now than half a century ago. Oh. And, actually, no one knows why the decreasing population is decreasing … or indeed why the increasing ones increase. Why do we hear otherwise? Our urban environmentalists have only ever seen a polar bear in a photo, and it's cute. It makes a great poster child for their cause. It does things for fund-raising that a walrus or an arctic char just wouldn't do.

- Regarding hurricanes: Katrina was opportune, dramatic, fated to happen, and a PR triumph or disaster, depending on your purpose. But it had *nothing* to do with Global Warming. GW did not set New Orleans below sea level or make the public administration of the city and of the state of Louisiana massively corrupt and ineffective, the real causes of the disaster. Moreover, one must expect a certain number of hurricanes on the Gulf Coast of the United States, and statistically, a few of these will be larger and stronger storms. In fact, the record shows that the number of Atlantic-Caribbean-Gulf hurricanes over the last twenty years is *less* (annual average) than in the previous fifty years. Oh. Moreover, did anyone notice that in the years subsequent to Katrina, our National Hurricane Center, our climate wonks, and Al Gore all got hot and bothered—frantic, really—about how there were going to be ever more hurricanes, ever more powerful, ever more destructive ... but there weren't? Once again, Mother Nature stuck her tongue out. Did these clowns retract one word of what they had said? Not a bit, not at all. They just went on to the next doomsday prediction without missing a beat, as if nothing at all had happened. But what happened is this: they got *every part* of their prediction *wrong.* Why is that important? Because there is a pattern, a pattern of failed predictions, of commercial success (they sell their snake oil), and of renewed prognostications of disasters, with each proposed calamity worse than the last. It's country fair time: bring in the rubes and snooker them. Look, if I sell tire chains, I favor snowy forecasts. If, like Al Gore, I am trying to make my next fortune in carbon- trading schemes, I need environmental catastrophes to promote them. We must never forget P. T. Barnum's words: "There is a sucker born every minute." As we say in New Hampshire, ayuh.
- Are summers getting hotter? Well, in some regions, summers are hot. But this means normally hot, with considerable year-to-year and day-to-day variability. Temperature "records" have been set in different places since we began measuring temperatures. Is it also a record if temperatures on an individual day do not set a record? Yes, if it's so for an extended period. On that basis, we

have a plethora of records. Sometime in the 1990s much of the United States suffered a hotter than normal summer. One of the then-better-known newsweeklies—might have been *Time*, might have been *Newsweek*—maybe both, as they were so often given to symbiotic covers, dedicated one issue to the "ever hotter summers we would face, that the summer we had barely survived presaged the hell to come, and that we were all going to die." The last bit was correct, but only in the natural course of life, not from hot summers. In fact, Mother Nature once more stuck her tongue out, and the succeeding summers to this day have been very average. Oh. As these same newsweeklies were exercised in the 1970s about "the coming ice age," anyone with a memory just ignored them as one ignores supermarket tabloid stories about five-legged pigs.

- Regarding the heating in the tropics and subtropics, there have been absolutely astonishing predictions of potential/probable/certain (you choose) increases in temperatures for these zones of the planet. One notable prediction by Canadian GW "scientists" regarded a 14°F increase in average summer temperatures for the southeastern United States. One thing we know for certain is that these scientists flunked physics. It requires massive quantities of energy to heat moisture-laden air (humid air), and that is exactly what we find in the tropics and sub-tropics. This is why the temperature rarely exceeds 32°C at the equator but routinely attains 40°C to 45°C in the *dry* zones between 15 and 35 degrees north and south latitude. It is not possible to get such temperatures in humid regions. The energy to heat the air simply isn't there. The sun isn't hot enough. Great science, guys!

- Remember acid rain? All our forests were going to brown and die because of acid rain. Along the East Coast, it became a frenzy. There wasn't a governor who didn't campaign on the acid-rain plank: "I'll go to the Midwest and shut down those dirty power plants!" they thundered. Putting aside that they were going to do no such thing—there still are some laws—it made for good soapbox rhetoric, the usual swill of political campaigns. There was another problem: acid rain wasn't actually the culprit, but rather a then-yet-undiscovered parasite that had, as nature does, infested the trees. Once again, correlation isn't causation. But we had ourselves a fine frenzy, and if in the process a few votes changed hands, where was the harm? And once again the environmental groups just edged away, as from a man who has farted at a party.

- The decrease of snow on Kilimanjaro. This iconic mountain is regularly trotted out as evidence of GW. There are problems, however. The summit temperature has not been warming. On the contrary: it has declined slightly over the last twenty years. What has also declined is precipitation. Why? Deforestation has occurred around the base and the plain surrounding the mountain, as inhabitants gathered fuel. No forest, no moisture. No reservoir of moisture at the base, no precipitation at the summit. There, now—feel better? Plant trees. Just as an aside, it would be utterly unrealistic to expect the summit glacier of Kilimanjaro to be constant and unchanging. No glacier is.

- Glaciers, Alps, Andean Cordillera, Alaska, Himalaya, et al. We *know* one thing: glaciers come and go. We *do not know* why. At first blush it would be easy—but wrong—to equate glaciers with cold beyond the obvious that a temperature below $0°C$ is required to freeze water. There are in fact two plausible hypotheses concerning glaciers: one, that colder temperatures slow glacial melt and that the glacier grows by gaining mass in winter and losing less mass in summer. Maybe. Two, that warmer temperatures increase precipitation and that the extra snow input becomes more ice mass at a rate that exceeds the melt loss. Oh. It could also be both, depending upon the aforementioned (very) complex climatic variables. And, yes, we can also be reasonably sure that during an ice age, the earth is colder, whereas when it is ice-free it is warmer. We don't know what sets off an ice age. Theories include solar activity, the tilt of the Earth's axis, cosmic radiation, and massive volcanic explosions and meteor strikes throwing huge quantities of dust into the atmosphere. Or all. Or none. We don't know. A new view is that contrary to an earlier belief that the onset of glaciation is a long process, it is in fact something that might occur in a human lifetime or less. Ditto the beginning of an interglacial period, the end of the ice age. If you want climate change, that's climate change! Maybe we can get Big Al to move to another hemisphere and adjust the planet's tilt. But back to our glaciers. I'll mention something anecdotal. As a boy, I spent much time with my family in the Swiss Alps, and the glaciers were—for the most part—longer, broader, and whiter than today. Many—not all—have retreated. It is interesting that not all have retreated, and it's interesting that in retreating, many have revealed ancient artifacts—not from so long ago, but from Roman times—and old vegetation, tree stumps, and so on. The same has been observed in America's Pacific Northwest, in the Cascades, where the retreat of a glacier revealed an ancient forest that had been beneath the ice. What is all the more interesting, given the present concern with GW, is that environmental groups went nuts that the information about the forest under the ice was revealed … because it would give people "the wrong idea." Really? What would that be? That the greenies had been caught out—caught telling tales? The same thing happened in Switzerland. The greenies were not amused to have it known that a well-known pass, which ought to have been covered since and for all eternity with ice, had clearly been ice-free in Roman times. Shit!

• Greenland is interesting: its coastal ice is thinning, and the ice-cap ice is thickening, with a net gain in ice mass. Some sort of a warming—not necessarily atmospheric—could explain it. At sea level, there would be some ice loss, whereas in the interior, where it's always cold—really cold—there might be more snowfall. Another image of the GW crowd is icebergs calving from glaciers. It's a dramatic picture. But it tells us nothing. Calving can as easily lead to ice retreat as it can be a symptom of ice advance (as the ice sheet advances farther into the sea, it becomes weaker and less stable, and bergs calve). A very small area of the Antarctic has seen significant ice loss—the Antarctic Peninsula, 3 percent of the continent's land, which juts some 1,000 kilometers north (i.e., toward warmer latitudes) from the main body of the continent—while the great ice dome of Antarctica is thickening. The total volume of ice in Antarctica is increasing.

- Disappearing atolls are quite the scam. These island groups, ringed with coral, are by definition sea-level affairs, without any margin for error, so to speak. Have sea levels risen? Not that anyone can measure. The whole brouhaha is that "they might" or "they will," based on computer models. Ah. Meanwhile, the natives who call these islands home haven't missed a beat: they are owed money from all of us who made, well—okay—might make their island homes disappear beneath the sea. But keep your eye on the money, because that's what this is about. Will some island groups disappear over time? Absolutely. Could be a rising sea. Could also be subsidence. Ah, forgot about that one. And will new island groups be born? Yup, that too. That is life on our planet; it is about *change*. But one thing about coral atolls: the coral *adjusts* to the sea level, up and down. Oh.

Change brings us to the key we *must* grasp, or we are fated to be made fools of by our planet. Our planet is alive, a fantastic, ever-changing living body. Everything changes every day. The GW alarmists write the most perfect nonsense about 20 percent, 40 percent, or 80 percent of all species being "wiped out." Well, it will happen. It has happened many times before. It will happen again. Not right now, though. In the context of a temperate planet in an interglacial period, what happens is that species die off—become extinct—and species are born. One thing the alarmists cannot deal with is change. This is positively primitive, a Luddite instinct that won't go away, a view of the world as static. That's going to be a tough one. It is not static, never has been static, and will not be static until it dies, eons from now, in geologic and galactic time. So, these people who inconvenience their laundress every time something changes are going to have a very hard time of it. If they got out into the wilderness, away from their flat-screen TVs and their iPods, they might spend an evening under the starry canopy of the universe and *reflect*.

Not more than a month past, I read a frantic article in one of the

United Kingdom papers that some fish—it doesn't really matter which—was now showing up further north "than its range." If it's now further north, hasn't its range changed? Are these urban environmentalists even aware that the ranges of mammals, birds, fish, insects and plants are *constantly* changing? If they don't know this they oughtn't to even touch the subject. It's Joe the plumber doing neurosurgery!

Do environmentalists, so preoccupied with the tropical rain forests, know that before man's time, the Amazon basin was mostly savannah, with only copses of trees? Do they know that the Vikings settled a far more temperate Labrador than the one we know? Do they understand that the American Southwest was once *beneath* a warm sea? That the plain of the River Po is geologically in Africa? That the north magnetic pole has been—quite literally—all over the place?

If there is one constant for our majestic, lovely, and fascinating planet, it is change—change, change, change, all of the time. And until we can separate the extraordinary and continuous natural changes from the puny changes man can bring, we cannot with any sane probability claim anthropogenic causes.

A personal note, which will be overlooked by critics but to which I attach great importance:

I love nature. I ski, I hike, I climb mountains, I sail, and I spend all the time I can outdoors. I have been fortunate and traveled widely across the globe. I photograph nature. I admire wildlife, and I am in thrall to polar bears. I live in the country, surrounded by fields and forest and old stone walls, the hundred hills of my home. I watch nature's cycles with daily pleasure. I note that this fall, we are overrun by squirrels, a very normal spike in a rodent population. Other years, there are fewer. In my study a new kind of beetle is on the loose. This happens at this season in northern New England: a few warm days seem to bring insects out from the walls, some known to us, and some much less so. I am an obdurate advocate of lucent waters, clean air, good forestry, careful wildlife management, and conservation. I am also modern. I have traveled enough to have seen that prosperity—and only prosperity—protects the environment. I have seen enough of human misery in countries where the state is overbearing and the people thus poor to know that free markets and liberty manumit us from wretchedness. I have been able to compare the quality of life and the care for nature under socialist regimes and under free-market regimes. There is no comparison, the former dingy and forlorn, the latter kempt and promising. The only person who can think otherwise has never traveled or is an arrogant rich kid who wants to keep the world's poor as his zoo animals, frozen in time in a cage. Silly magazines as the once reputable but now entirely politicized National Geographic send their rich kid reporters to dismal places, and they return reporting how happy the natives are to be living in earthen huts and cooking over dung fires, living the traditional life. Bosh! They are malnourished, eking out some kind of subsistence from poorly managed lands, denied markets by rich-world farm subsidies, importuned by corrupt, thieving tyrants, suffering from a host of diseases we would easily treat ...and dying. These rich-kid reporters are immoral, satisfying their urban-social adolescent dreams, refusing to grow up even as the years pass. Their causes, based on false science and priggish spoiled habits, kill human beings. Several environmental groups, one the very well-known WWF, which have very slickly packaged themselves, are greatly exercised, for example, about "indigenous peoples" in the Indonesian rain forest, all one thousand of them, but would sacrifice 400,000 Indonesians who depend on forestry for their and their families' livelihoods. We aren't speaking of wealth here; we're speaking of eating. Only the rich of the world, the rich and unconscious and unconscionable, can act this way. If they had any sense, they would know that only prosperity can bring solutions to many of the concerns they have, as only prosperity—or famine—can control population growth. In the world's developed nations there is more forest today than a century ago! Prosperity is the key, not a return to primitive, miserable existences. If these environmentalists believed what they say, rather than just playacting it in an endless puerile tantrum, they would go off and live in wilderness huts, scrounging for food, weakened by parasitic diseases, cold when it's cold, hot when it's hot, and wet when it's wet. And stay there! Not a week, not a month, not a year "for the experience." No, no, no! Stay here, and die young—like the natives, like the poor!

It is time the grown-ups took charge again.

Now come. It's time to put aside the angry words. Draw up a chair by the fire and we'll speak of the skies over Connemara, perchance of the poetry of Pasternak. I found a ripe Cashel Blue at the cheese shop, and I just happen to have this wonderful bottle of '89 Haut-Brion. We'll drink it together.

Postscript to Chapter 6

As I was writing Chapter 6 of this book, the story broke that hackers, or perhaps a whistle-blower, had gotten into the servers of the University of East Anglia (UK) Climate Center, one of the key centers in the world for the advancement of the global-warming hypothesis. Indeed the climate center allowed itself to be converted into an activist hub. The hackers posted over one thousand e-mails between global- warming advocates—the scientists who named themselves to the "all scientists agree" clan—which show, taken together, that at a minimum, there has been much awry in the behavior of these scientists. If what appears to be true, based on those e-mails, were confirmed, they would no longer have the right to be called scientists. It is as though hackers had penetrated the servers of the Vatican and discovered e-mails between the pope and his cardinals showing that they doubt the divinity of Christ, that they had hidden new evidence of his mortality, and that they had falsified documents to cynically maintain his divinity.

As is usual in this age of information technology, and we address the risk to all of our privacies from IT later in this book, nothing remains secret forever. If teenagers can hack into the Pentagon, they can surely get into the University of East Anglia.

Now the fun has begun. The skeptics who have been so vilified for so long are tasting victory. The environmental groups have gone into full Nixon mode: burning and deleting files, placing the most tenuous interpretations on words, representing that "tricking the numbers" doesn't mean what it says, and pulling out all the stops with their fellow conspirators in the media. Articles so similar in content and phrase that they can only emanate from a single source have popped up in major newspapers, announcing ever more ludicrous end-of-the-world scenarios. Next we shall be told that GW will revive long- dormant Tyrannosaurus rex DNA, and the great beasts will run amok across the planet, ghoulishly feasting on small babies—and with luck radical environmentalists—as Cyclops in *The Aeneid*. Be afraid, be very afraid, or Al Gore will bore you to death. So it is with houses of cards and sand castles; they do in the end fall and crumble.

In the ramp-up to the Copenhagen Climate Summit, due just ten days hence from this writing, we will see the battle lines drawn. At the summit the extreme warning scenarios will become hysterical—in both senses of the word—and it wouldn't be surprising to see some of the rats jumping ship. It will only take one or two of these policy conspirators— can't really call them scientists anymore—turning coat and trying to save themselves with a snarling accusation toward their colleagues of "I told you so" or an "I never agreed, but …" and we shall have ourselves what some have already baptized Climate-gate. Moreover, the hackers must be working on the next juicy hit. The radical environmentalists are getting back some of their own, after having long pretended that their breaking of laws, their exaggerations, and their outright lies were justified by the Good Cause. Curious that they have now become sticklers for the law, castigating the hackers' illegal act! Wiser men know that most blades cut both ways.

What we shall also see will be a rapid morphing of the myth. Some of these prestidigitators will quietly—but quickly, yes ma'am, faster than you can see the hand—substitute other causes for the fatally stricken Global Warming Beast. These causes will always have the same common thread: anti-enterprise socialism. The free market will be bad for you. With any luck, the people, having been made the butt of a monumental fraud, will for a time be chastened and wary. If our intuition that what underlies the hysteria that global warming became is a crisis of spirituality, we must expect that some new deity will be soon enough wheeled in to replace the fallen GW.

I propose to leave these words as I have written them, come what may. It would be Icarian to believe in one view to the exclusion of all others; thus I am prepared to accept whatever may ultimately out. Kipling said this best when he advised his son to keep his head about him while others are losing theirs, but to leave room for their doubting. An interesting development, this East Anglia thing.

Chapter 7
The Profit Motive vs. the Trough Motive

I have a friend, a man of uncommon education and intelligence, who has—as I suppose we all do—a blind spot. He is an academic. Perhaps I do not need to say more. Coming from his lips, the word "profit" is an accusation. This is so common and so pernicious a thing that it merits all of our attention. There are so many misapprehensions about profit, held at all levels of society and at all levels of education, that this can only derive from a removal from the land.

As our wealthy societies have increasingly mechanized agriculture, very few of us remain "on the land." We do not earn our daily bread with our hands in the soil, and we have no clue at all about many things with which Grandfather and Grandmother grew up. Most of us would be hard pressed to survive if we had to grow something to feed ourselves, if we had to milk a cow, or if we had to kill a rabbit for a stew. The statistics tell us that although 4 percent of Americans farm, only half this many feed us; the others farm for their pleasure. The latter are surely hardworking, but economically speaking, they are dilettantes.

We have grown far from the land. From an economic standpoint, it's a good thing, but every gain has a loss. Our urban dwellers no longer understand the land. A few years ago a movement got under way in the UK to ban what they call hunting, what we call fox hunting to hounds. The cry was "Animal cruelty!" but the purpose was very different.

It might have been Swift who said, "The Puritans don't oppose bear baiting because it's cruel to an animal, but because it gives pleasure to men." There is more truth to this than a passing smile. As the antihunting campaign gathered steam, it became all too apparent that the cry against cruelty to animals was a veil for something rather more ugly: class warfare. By the time the bill passed into law, the deceit was out; some of its leading advocates had been heard openly to say, "It's about the toffs." Many kind, ordinary English people had been gulled by the animal-cruelty claim. They had been used. And the reason they could be used is that they no longer lived on the land. Had they been nearer the land, they would have known that foxes are a plague to husbandry, and that farmers—in the protection of the fowl and livestock they raise, *which we will eat*—shoot, trap, and poison foxes. Well, the laborites who pressed the antihunting campaign on an innocent *urban* nation never spoke of the cruelty of shooting, trapping and poisoning foxes. I'm going somewhere with this; follow me please.

The campaign was no more than a cheap attack on a pleasure seen by obdurate urban socialists as too aristocratic. Urban dwellers, knowing not the land, were sucker punched. Now, some years on, following Lincoln's dictum that you can't fool all of the people all of the time, there is a widespread recognition that the ban is without merit. It will soon be overturned.

George McGovern, the once-upon-a-time socialist candidate for the presidency—yes, I know, we don't call politicians that over here, but he was—subsequently came to give up politics, showing us that he was at least a decent man. With his wife, he bought a country inn, I think in Connecticut, imagining a genteel semi-retirement living by a venerable, peaceable trade. By his own confession he had a very hard time of it, and to his great credit came to declare, "If I had known when I served in the Senate what I know now, I would never have voted for many of the measures I did."

This is the problem with profit; it is the modern-day "land," and too many of us are too far from it, so we disdain or misunderstand it from ignorance. For many the last profit they earned was at a childhood roadside lemonade stand, as good a business model as ever was: Mom and Dad provide the facilities and the product, and the child pockets the remarkable 100 percent profit. One more anecdote, if you will.

Years ago—it was the time of the government-caused petroleum crisis of 1974—a young, bright, not-unattractive California attorney angrily challenged me at a party: "Don't you think it's just absurd that the petroleum companies are earning over 100 percent profits?" Absurd indeed, ma'am.[4] The lack of basic economic literacy—the distance of modern man from the new "land"—leads to grievous public-policy errors and to a return to an invidious envy in society that can only ultimately mislead us.

When more of us earned our livings by small trades—selling vegetables at the weekly market; cobbling shoes; peddling buttons; taking in laundry; shoeing horses; beekeeping; thatching—the notion of profit was more natural, instinctive, and unsophisticated. Profit was in our pockets, not on a ledger. There was nothing arcane about it, and surely nothing insidious. It was no more than a man's living. But it was profit, for without profit we cannot live.

Academics have a hard time with this, believing as they do that they are remunerated by some magical instance ... and too little to boot, given their opinion of the light they think to bring. The reality is that their wages are paid either by taxpayers—thus, money seized by the state from their fellow citizens; or by tuition—money earned by the labor of their students (or more likely their students' parents); or by donations and grants—so, money first earned as a profit. They sell themselves for profit, but pretend otherwise, that their salaries are paid by some unidentified act of benevolence. As those who eat meat but who could not bear to kill an animal, they are a bit squeamish regarding how it all comes about. I am only harsh with a purpose, to demonstrate that even academics who would have us believe that they live without

---

4   I feel the need—proving my case once again—to explain to my academic friends the irony of the response: a profit in excess of 100 percent is a mathematical impossibility, as profit is measured as a percentage of revenue. Although, come to think of it, a government subsidy could create such an absurdity ... that's what old T. Boone was looking for with those propeller towers.

eating, eat as the rest of us. Profit needs to be gotten into as cold water: progressively. First some general information:

- The average profit earned by all businesses across America is less than 7 percent. This means that when we pay one dollar for a thing, 93 cents are the cost of the thing, and 7 cents are the seller's profit. Does that seem unreasonable, to pay a man 7 cents of every dollar to bring us a product or a service? In survey after survey, people get this massively wrong when polled. They come up with percentages that are completely off the mark: 50 percent is quite a common guess, and 20 percent to 90 percent is a not-uncommon range. Almost no one who does not run a business, large or small, guesses that the real number is less than 10 percent.

- Well, okay, regarding the 7 percent, I don't know where you got that, and I don't really believe ya. Why, you only have to look at a company like Chrysler! They took so much profit out of it that now they're bankrupt. You smile. You think I'm kidding. But we are so far from the "land" that this is something people say. Another common remark is that a rich man made a business fail "for the tax loss." Only if he can't count.[5] Another common canard is that a business is failing, but "they're just hiding the money." Oh. So, the shareholders lose their investment, and lose the engine of profit they had hoped to create; some lose the homes they had mortgaged to invest in the business; but they're just hiding the money. Funny—they didn't bring it out to prevent the foreclosure! European labor unions long believed this and would make economically impossible demands on their employers, sending them into bankruptcy. The notion was always the same. They were being lied to, and in fact there was

---

5   Again, for my academic friends: a tax loss is deductible from taxable income, within specified parameters. It does not make you money. It *saves* you some money by allowing you to offset some gain with some loss, e.g., if you earn $100 selling banana bread—sorry, this needs to be kept simple for academics—and lose $40 selling oranges, most would agree that you have only earned $60. This is the principle of tax loss. Now, I ask you: would you not rather have earned $100 with the bread and another $40 with the oranges? You'd have $140 for your trouble instead of $60. Wouldn't that make more sense than a tax loss?

plenty of money. Our unions, and to be fair some European ones too, now, have become much more sophisticated over the last three decades and understand the company's books as well as management does. When times are tough, they're tough, it's real, and everyone tightens his belt. It's a far more sensible approach than the almost feudal belief that the lord of the manor "always has money," never mind the leaking roof he cannot repair.

- Profit is the fair and necessary reward for risk. Without profit there is no reason for anyone to invest. The economy stalls. If a tax, as Frédéric Bastiat showed, takes from everyone, a profit gives to everyone. I have set out two distinct asseverations, and I shall take them up individually. If you can get a 4 percent tax-free income from municipal bonds, and you have $100,000 to invest, then without effort or risk you could earn $4,000 per year. Now, suppose a friend came to you with a plan to establish a car wash in town, and promised you $4,000 a year for your $100,000 investment. Would you invest? Not unless you're more foolish than I think.

- Okay, so what would your friend need to show you to get you to take your money from the municipal bond and put it into the car wash? Well, first he has to show you enough profit that you'll be level with the bond *after tax*. If you pay taxes at a 30 percent rate, this means $5,715. Would that get you into the car-wash business? Not likely. You'd only get $4,000 after tax—same as the bond—and that's *if* the business went well. But you know it might not—nine out of ten new businesses fail—even though your friend is a good guy. So, what would you need to get out of the bond? At what point does the potential *reward* compensate for the *risk*? I'd think you'd want at least a reasonable prospect of 50 percent more than the bond, after tax. You'd have to be looking at $8,570 before tax to move your money. Oh, that's an 8.57 percent profit. At some point, at some level of projected profit, the reward will outweigh the risk for you, and you'll invest in the car wash. Two things will happen: the people in town will have a new service available to them, and if everything goes well and you do make the extra money—above the interest income you had on the bond—you'll have more money to spend, or to invest. *The profit will have given to everyone:* the people with cleaner cars, the housepainter to whom you gave an extra job, and the milliner from whom your wife bought a new coat. This simple notion is little understood. Those who have studied philosophy will recognize Adam Smith.

• Adam Smith was, for our daily bread, the most important philosopher of the last three centuries—one could say of the Enlightenment. It is worthwhile to repeat his famous words, "It is not from the benevolence of the butcher, the brewer, or the baker that we expect our dinner, but from their regard for their own interest. We address ourselves not to their humanity but to their self-love." Also, "It is the greatest impertinence and presumption, therefore, in kings and ministers to pretend to watch over the economy of private people, and to restrain their expense … They are themselves always, and without any exception, the greatest spendthrifts in society." Finally: "Every individual necessarily labors to render the annual revenue of the society as great as he can. He generally indeed neither intends to promote the public interest, nor knows how much he is promoting it. He intends only his own gain, and he is in this, as in many other cases, led by an invisible hand to promote an end which was no part of his intention. By pursuing his own interest he frequently promotes that of the society more effectually than when he really intends to promote it. I have never known much good done by those who affected to trade for the public good." Adam Smith cannot be sufficiently reread. George McGovern learned his Adam Smith the hard way. He would have done us more good in the Senate had he come by the lesson sooner. Our politicians, today increasingly professional politicians who have never earned a cent but by sucking on the public teat, have no idea, no clue at all.

It is worthwhile to inquire, philosophically, into the nature of profit. What is this thing called profit? It is the benefit we hope to gain from the investment of our labor. Only the most unreformed Maoist would deny a man that.

Do we begrudge a mom-and-pop store its profit at the end of the year? No. Why not? What distinguishes it from the profit of Exxon-Mobil, which nine out of ten academics will tell you is in some unspecified way "evil"? It's the amount, isn't it? But economically speaking the only just measure of a profit is a percentage, not an amount. If the store is earning a 12 percent profit with sales of $400,000, it makes $48,000 pretax, and everybody is okay with that. But let Exxon-Mobil earn 4 percent on $50 billion, thus $2 billion pretax, and many will speak of Exxon-Mobil's "huge profit" or even "obscene profit," if it's in one of the silly newspapers. Well, it's not. In our example, the store would in fact be earning a strong profit, Exxon-Mobil a weak one. Indeed, a business that consistently earns a 4 percent pretax net *does not earn enough to justify further investment.*

The entire field of business numbers seems to defy the understanding of most journalists. We routinely see sales confused with earnings, for example. This would be as wrong as confusing what you earn with what you save. For most of us these are very different numbers. When we get to distinctions between profit, profit after tax, return on investment, and return on assets, utter perplexity reigns. The journalists have no clue. It matters because they randomly and recklessly bandy these figures about, getting them all backward, and thus misinform public opinion. Consider, for instance, two ways of announcing the Exxon-Mobil profit spoken of here above: first, "Exxon-Mobil posts weak results, pretax net down to 4 percent, investors concerned," or second, "Exxon-Mobil earns huge $2 billion profit."

Let us examine yet another facet of profit, one also too readily overlooked. Who earns it? Economically speaking the question is this: can a company earn a profit? Not really. The profit is earned by the shareholders individually, which in our economy means that the profit of many of our largest companies is owned by many thousands of individual investors—hundreds of thousands, in fact, through investments made by pension funds, endowments, and other institutional investors. I once had a surreal discussion with a friend who judged herself—and honestly was—an able small investor. She and her husband weren't wealthy, just solid middle-class Americans looking to increase their retirement kitty. In a single conversation, she spoke to me of her investments in pharmaceutical stocks "because they performed well," and of the "immoral price gouging" by pharmaceutical firms. Nothing—nothing short of a brain transplant, I think—could make her understand that *she* was the price gouger. I hope you'll agree that this is in the "it follows as night the day" category, the only conclusion possible from her affirmations. But no, the companies were evil, and she was innocent. Well, in one sense of the word I suppose she was innocent.

An academic with a smattering of economics and a few words idly collected from an annual report—probably while perusing the return of his pension fund—will retort, "Ah, but you are overlooking retained earnings; that's where the evildoers salt it all away." Uh, no. Retained earnings are as a savings account, and a company can do only two things with the saved money: reinvest it in the company or pay it out to shareholders. Both benefit the wider world. It cannot be otherwise. A company—a corporation—is a free association of labor and capital that can only act as a *pass-through* for money. Investors place money in the company, which is used to buy productive assets or to pay wages; individuals who are employed by the company exchange their labor for money. A corporation does not have a mattress under which to stuff money. The government, in its boundless deceitfulness and unwisdom, has also compelled corporations to become a conduit for taxes, in order to *conceal* from the people the full amount of taxes they pay. We'll speak of that later.

Finally, I think the problem many have with profit is that they simply do not understand mathematics: how many can unhesitatingly write out "two billion, five hundred and fifty three million, four hundred and twenty two thousand, six hundred and thirty six" in numerals? Ask around. You'll see. When we understand that our government now casually speaks of trillions, we come to understand the problem. So these numbers become undifferentiated vast sums in the public mind, the ugly colloquialism "humongous" used as the catch-all. And if it's humongous, it's just too damned much—in fact, it's obscene. No attempt to relate the number to percentages will prove successful. Our high-school education is too poor for that anymore. The man in the street only vaguely understands a percentage, usually as "50 percent off" in a post-Christmas sale, but is unable to relate it to other uses, as in the understanding of relative values. A lady of my near acquaintance routinely repeats to me that "military spending is the major part of our budget," and the information that it is in fact 28 percent is without intellectual effect.

This all matters because *profit is the engine of our prosperity.* Profit enables us to invest in all the things we desire. Without profit there is no money for the environment. No money for education. No money for home repairs. No money for groceries. No money. Not a penny. Not a half-pence. None.

This brings us to the bête noir of those who no more understand economics than they understand astrophysics: the despised "profit motive." But they too have this mean streak. It is why they work. The profit motive is the natural human desire to eat, to house oneself, to provide a better life for one's kids, to buy a new car, to give something to charity, to get ahead. There are a few who think all of these uncontrolled consumerism, but these are a fringe bringing together naiveté in youth, discontent in middle age, and toothless anger in life's autumn. They will blame the profit motive for every evil under the sun. Do power plants pollute? Blame the profit motive, never mind that our unhappy friends use electricity. Are newspapers—the paper, you see—cutting down our forests? Blame the profit motive, never mind that they read the paper themselves. Does the discount toaster break? Blame the profit motive, never mind that a good quality toaster was next to the cheap one on the shelf. It is a completely childish disavowal of responsibility. Every ill of society is the fault of corporations and the profit motive, and nothing is the responsibility of the consumer. The consumer is seen as an ingénue of extravagant proportions, unable to not buy the newspaper or to live without electricity. She sees herself somehow compelled to do these things by dark forces beyond her ken or control.

My words, I know, will have no effect on those who see in the profit motive the cynosure of evil in this world. I cannot change them. It's an article of faith. They will reflexively judge that what is private and profit-driven is bad, and what is public and pointless is good. They confuse motives with result, failing to comprehend the simple logic of Adam Smith. So, as we cannot win this battle, allow me to suggest, in all fairness, an equivalent term for public employment and spending: the trough motive.

When a man tells you how he is honest but his fellow is not, keep your pockets tight, for he is liar and likely a thief. Unlike some effects in particle physics, wherein the particles sort themselves into patterns, men do not. Our common experience informs us that there are as many honest as dishonest people in most villages, towns, and cities; in most occupations; in most of the divisions we make in our society. That a man is a Republican or a Democrat tells us nothing about his honesty or dishonesty. One can be as the other. The notion that somehow those who do not labor in the hope of private gain, but who feed upon public funds, are more honest than their fellows is born I think of the suspicion the dull have of the clever. Unable to understand how a neighbor does better than he, the dunce suspects sleight of hand. To admit his limitation wouldn't do. But the trough motive in our social democracies has become an apparently uncontrollable economic force. We may judge by our ever more bloated budgets. Nor are those who anoint themselves in self-proclaimed good works immune from the trough motive. It is well-known that in universities our academics direct their inquiries to paths which are more likely to secure grants, and all the self-congratulatory folk in the NGOs who seek to manipulate our world prostitute themselves to donations. The trough motive: there's a Nobel Prize in economics to be gained here!

Are we to detail the evidence? Is there anyone in a Western social democracy who does not understand how politicians and functionaries help themselves? Do we need to remind our European friends of their newborn aristocracy in Brussels, who have awarded themselves *tax-free* status? In an act of breathtaking arrogance, these scoundrels, who have never seen a tax they didn't judge fit for their citizens—their serfs is more like it—*exempted* themselves from the payment of taxes!

In the UK, the nation has just been through a great scandal, from which we learned that their politicians were using public allowances, mostly legally to boot, to do the vital business of the kingdom—things such as employing family, reroofing their houses, doing mortgage swaps so the taxpayer ended up paying for their private residences, taking trips abroad, gardening, entertaining mistresses and lovers, and all the titillating bits. Good stuff. Need I say more?

In the United States, the politicians award themselves ever higher salaries and the benefits of princes while the nation suffers the highest unemployment rate in decades. The trough motive: it hardly requires a long itemization. We have only to go to our nearest politician—pick one, any one—to find him gorging on public largesse.

If we move over to our campuses, we have only to check out who gets grants and who doesn't; the ones who do pray to the full pantheon of politically correct gods. Those who don't go empty-handed. The choice is stark: sell yourself and squeal happily with all the other swine, or don't and become bacon. Ditto the NGOs, those self-declared angels riding about on their white horses, many benefiting from a status as charities when they are by any definition PACs, fulfilling the adolescent caprices of spoiled brats and feeding off well-intentioned but uninformed donations and government grants.

But these sins are no more than peccadilloes when it comes to really snorting the swill. The Big One, as we have already examined, is the pork in all of our Western democracies' budgets, the calculated and conscious buying of votes. If they would forbear that, we should be glad to pay them in world cruises—the longer and farther the better! But in fact that is the very thing they will never agree to give up: the pork that keeps them in power.

And *we* are guilty. It is we who allow ourselves to be suborned, to be as shamelessly used as the lowest prostitute, to be their serfs and their chattel. How many months of the year did *you* work for them? Oh, sure, we all know there are legitimate common expenses. We aren't speaking of those. We're speaking of massive amounts of money, our money, handed out to whomever they care to give it, wherever they think they can gather some votes. We're speaking of a recently awarded two hundred and fifty bucks to all social-security recipients in the United States, thirteen billion dollars all in. Why? Because they weren't going to get cost-of-living increases this year. Know why? Because the cost of living didn't increase. And none of us who works is getting any cost of living increase, either. Vote buying, pure and simple.

It would be wrong, however, to focus our ire on one or the other major party. This is now a circus that has attained critical mass. There is no want that will not be satisfied, no vote left unbought.

Any fair study of the last one hundred years makes one thing clear: free markets work, socialism doesn't. The profit motive ought to be the white knight, the trough motive pilloried. However, deep within us we have the notion that what is earned must be shady but what is given—the obverse of which is taken—must be good. We can despair of getting that across, even if China is making a fair stab at it. So let us at least despair and vilify equally: let us install the trough motive in its rightful house of shame!

A further thought: When one presses the point, it is common to find one's dissenting interlocutor throwing up the financial scandals of the private sector. The word "greed" often appears. I leave it to the reader to decide whether greed is not the operative impulse in the trough motive. But critics of the market inevitably overlook the truth that scandals may exist in the private sector, but these scandals are ineluctably connected to the public sector, either through cynical largesse, inane regulations, government grants and licenses, or overt political favoritism. Government is often at the root of the scandal. Many of us believe that the massive bailouts of the 2008–2009 period, under first a Republican and then a Democrat administration, represent one of the grossest examples of corruption the republic has ever suffered. Government by force took money honestly earned, by the labor of tens of millions of citizens, and gave it to bloated and mismanaged companies. Those who had run their affairs well were rewarded by getting the bill! This is making the sober pay for the drunks. We have not even begun to pay what this will ultimately cost. The lesson taught the reckless and the shameless may be the most expensive of all: we, an indulgent citizenry, will bail you out. Ford Motor Company, who asked no money, have the privilege of paying taxes to fund the propping up of their longtime competitor General Motors, one of the worst managed major companies of modern times. The market would have rightly suffered GM to die. Ford or Toyota or Volkswagen could have picked up the remains for what they were worth—not much—and made something of them, at no cost to us. Instead the government decided GM should live. We who pay the bill weren't asked. If public opinion polls are to be believed, we would have said no. This is increasingly the inclination of our all-powerful governments, to damn the citizen. The UK was taken into the unholy alliance known as the European Union by a conspiracy of politicians who would not submit the abandonment of British sovereignty to the people. Of course they couldn't. Every poll showed the people would have voted it down two-to-one. The British citizen has been emasculated without consultation. This is the trend of the Western social democracies, to have increasingly powerful and detached governments make the most vital decisions by diktat.

Where there is government there is corruption. I give you the trough motive!

Chapter 8
Manners, Ethics, and iPods

This Chapter is no more than a cry in the wilderness. More likely it is what a high-school teacher long ago admonished me against, railing at the gods. It doesn't matter. A man unjustly facing the firing squad may be granted a last statement, a *cri de coeur*, something that proclaims even before the awful finality of eternity, "I am a man; I was here." It may be utterly pointless, a discordant note as soon sung as carried off by the wind, but still it must be said: the iPod generation are awful brats.

One generation never entirely understands the next. That is the way of the world, and it is as it ought to be, with each successive generation pushing the limit in its own way. Nothing, however, excuses bad manners. The iPod kids have infected us all, and good manners are seen as a fusty anachronism. They are not. The only reason the kids have gotten away with it thus far is one with grave long-term implications: they do have a telegraph-like form of contact and so are able to exchange bits of information, the now-electronic grunts of primitive man. It is done all in pieces, a rough agglomeration of half-formed, and *half-thought*, phrases. They have created around themselves an aura of technology, of multitasking, of cool, of the future. In reality, they are far less efficient than their grandparents. They never get anything entirely done. It's all fractured.

Anecdotally I recount the following. I had an experience with a major company in 2009 in which a high-tech team of kids—okay, young managers, officially, although none displayed the least managerial savvy—proved unable to accomplish in three months what a plodding pro of old would have done—by himself—in a morning's work. The project was so poorly managed by these kids that it ultimately failed, having consumed many hundreds of hours and a large sum of money. What happened?

- Not one of them had time to ever complete a single meeting, to actually *listen* to anyone else, whether colleague or vendor.
- No discussion could ever occur without incessant interruption by Blackberry, mobile phone, or human intrusion, with the result that what was said was not understood.
- Nothing was ever recorded, preventing any orderly review of a discussion after the fact or any ordering of thoughts.
- Vital decisions could not be made—in fact a complete paralysis reigned on this front—because the need for the decision was not understood, and the information underlying it not registered.
- By seeking to handle half a dozen projects simultaneously, to appear "with it," the kids handled none to completion.
- Simple communications, such as questions requiring replies for any progress to be made, were left unattended and unanswered. (One of our managers gained access—legitimately—to one of the kids' laptops and found why no information was forthcoming; the kid was not opening most of his e-mails.)
- Promised return calls, promised deadlines, and promised information all failed to appear. Conference calls organized days in advance for a precise time with named participants would connect us, the vendor, to empty space; the kids just did not show and then did not apologize for not showing, not once or twice, but repeatedly.
- Anything that went wrong was blamed on others. Nothing was ever their fault. If we as the vendor insisted that we required specific information to meet their requirements—minor things,

you understand, such as how many, when, and where—we "lacked flexibility" or "didn't understand how they worked."

- No one had the confidence to assume the leadership role, nor did anyone have the experience to substitute a consensus for the missing leadership; everything got pushed around, and nothing was acted upon.
- You get the gist. Interestingly the solution of the kids, having failed to effect a very simple transaction, was to go back to a vendor who they themselves had declared "hopeless." I am allowed to think that this may not have been the case.

These kids were not, deep down, bad kids. If one spoke to them a little, scratched the surface a bit, one found rather ordinary kids: potentially nice kids who were very unsure of themselves, easily angered in the face of frustration, and culturally rude. I should add that while I can only call them kids—their comportment allows no other consideration—their ages ranged from the mid-twenties to the late thirties, so not children. In another time one would have expected responsibility. Point One.

Two: observe young parents of about the same age group as here above when they travel—now, as often as not in business class, with their screaming offspring. They occupy space without any regard for their neighbors. The children are left to do whatever they will do, ignored or admired by their oblivious or fawning parents, and the parents, dressed as for the gym, blithely exposing bellies and buttocks, just get on with things without even attempting to consider the comfort of fellow travelers. They inhabit a closed, encapsulated world. It is a world without communication. The parents did what one must do to procreate—let us charitably suppose that this was as for previous generations—but seem otherwise to communicate, even between themselves, by a sort of truncated code. As soon as possible, they cut themselves off from each other, plugging in and tuning out with whatever electronic device they carry. Now, it is true that all couples since time began have had moments of chill between them, but this isn't that: it's simply people in the habit of occupying isolated cubicles in space and time who have lost the capacity to communicate. And now it's spreading to their elders: isolation is the new cool!

Three: the insular notion of self surely diminishes one's regard for, consideration of, and civility toward others. In fact we see just this happening. The daily interactions once lubricated with small courtesies have been replaced by a staccato form that is about *me*, about what *I* want, about *my* need, and yours be damned. How, in fact, did we come to consider it anything less than rude to address a correspondent—even if in an e-mail—with the blunt "Joe" or "Tanya"? What happened to the "Dear" required by good manners? Is it really too long to write, or does courtesy now somehow seem to us too intimate, a violation of our isolation capsule? Some have tried to substitute "Hi" in a vestigial nod to etiquette, the "Dear" having fallen into desuetude, ringing euphuistically. Soon there will be no form of address at all, with perhaps "Hey you" as an interim measure.

Do we not lose something when the refinements of life are lost? The author Ursula Zilinsky wrote, "Civilization is the making of pleasures of life's necessities—food, shelter, and sex." It's as good a definition as any. Surely we can feed ourselves from a bowl, with our hands for utensils; no doubt we can inhabit an accommodation unit, Churchill's sardonic gibe in mind; and it goes without saying we might couple in the alley behind the Greek restaurant or in front of city hall, as do dogs ... but do we not lose something when we do? Is it not agreeable to be civil? Does it not make life easier on us?

Today, if one spends a nice evening out in any of our major cities—New York, London, Paris—one must expect to be thrown into a sort of washer-dryer of assorted laundry, the standard of fashion apparently established by a midnight raid upon the wardrobe of Eliza Doolittle in *My Fair Lady*. At the opera, having invited one's wife for an anniversary, and said wife having had the pleasure of it and taken trouble with her toilette, it is not improbable that one's neighbor will be in torn jeans and an old pullover: in your face. Is it to be a snob to wish for an elegant evening out? Short of attending privately organized galas—which always have a Westminster Dog Show air about them—there is no elegance left in our world, certainly none reliable. It's the same in nice—and not inexpensive—restaurants. Anything goes.

It is the iPod brats. They want to go everywhere in their grubby jeans, because the world is about them. It's a Ptolemaic universe with an ego at its center. No public space is closed to this rabble. They navigate the globe in their running shoes and make a point of their bad manners; really, they insist. If I sound terribly old-fashioned, it is willful; I see no reason to like a world of physical and intellectual grunginess. The physical grunginess lies beneath the sheets with an attitude of indifference that values only the comfort of the moment. It engenders a mental grunginess. It's a world lived "for me" and "for the instant." There are few values. Already, we see a redefining of honesty. It has become a little quaint. The iPod kids think honesty is whatever they say it is. So by their lights, they are honest. The reality is they no longer understand honesty, a notion in all societies connected with honor—and the good manners inseparable from it. It is absolutely routine today for someone who has pledged you a thing to later, for want of a signature, dismiss you with, "Do you have it in writing?"

Anecdotally, I experienced this in an exchange with a major Italian fashion house, at the highest levels. A word, a representation, is without value. Convenience is all. They do because they can, the legal systems of our social democracies having been corrupted to give every advantage to the wrongdoer while lining the pocket of the practitioner. The problem became so universal with these large international luxury brands, and obviously spoken of by suppliers, that the brands' own association put "dishonesty" on the agenda of a 2009 meeting!

Let's take a moment to think about this. If it is correct that an absence of manners, honor, and honesty is one part of a whole, this would readily explain the contemporary habit of rudeness and dishonesty. When Socrates said, "Man is the measure of all things," he never imagined it could come to mean "a man." He referred to man taken as a community. In an encapsulated world, in which each isolates himself from the other, even within families and within a marriage, there is no hope for good manners … or honesty.

I am not, however, entirely pessimistic. These things tend to go in cycles of culture and of fashion, and I expect to see a return to better manners, not perhaps because they are more agreeable—even if that would be reason enough—but because *bad manners don't work.* Man gave up his primitive coarseness because finding a smoother accord within society worked better. This was the birth of good manners. There were times when we went too far and developed manners of an extreme complication, pretension, and prissiness, as in the court of Louis XIV or in the insular evolution of Japanese society. But look at us today: men who ought to know very much better wearing their baseball caps to dinner, and I'm not speaking of an I-70 roadhouse. It doesn't even bear comment that these caps are worn indoors everywhere, a sort of badge that says "I am a man," or in Asia, "I'm cool," in that peculiarly geeky Asian way, where in the recent past it would have been only evidence of truly bad manners, the simplest of men knowing that a hat is removed upon entering a house.

None should mistake a call for decent manners for stuffiness or haughtiness. It is far more basic: a call for not ultimately murdering each other. If it can bring a certain agreeableness with it, a refinement of temper and habit, what can be against it?

Lynne Truss, in her book *Talk to the Hand,* speaks of the "utter bloody rudeness of everyday life." She is indignant, wry, sardonic, funny, and regretful, but ultimately also concerned that our loss of manners will be the worse for us. She too touches upon the unsuccessful mixing of the human and the mechanical, the automated systems that waste untold hours of *our* time to correct a matter of concern to us *as customers* in a system that wants us grateful for the seller's condescension while *we* favor him with *our* money.

That is, assuming the matter can even be corrected. I once spent half a year, long enough that I feel I now have jihad experience, trying to get fraudulent charges on a credit card sorted out. I won't run you through the house of horrors; everyone has his own version of the tale. Suffice it to say that the system appeared designed to prevent efficiency—in this regard it was enormously successful—and to discourage its use—again, a triumph, but leaving the client to feel angry, powerless, and apoplectic. Ha! You thought you could get through the maze, didn't you? But you can't!

Most distressing is what seems to be a calculated abnegation of responsibility by the managements of the firms concerned, unless the explanation lies in a dullness of intellect that would embarrass an Irish Setter. Isn't this simply corporate rudeness automated? What is different in this wring cycle from the village merchant who is gruff and unaccommodating?

We have one so rude in our town that his shop is known sarcastically as "the charm school." What is much harder to account is that people continue to give him their custom. They just take it. We just take it, ordered inconsiderately about by anyone with a mop and a tinsel of authority. Pressed, pressed too hard, we retaliate: eff off! The target is oblivious. He is not connected to our world, to our space, to our time, by any filament of common decency. We might as well have been the dog lifting his leg against a hydrant. The hydrant knows not and cares not.

In the UK, we will be manhandled by the force of law for having "treated our personnel in an abusive manner." Imagine that! The bastards do a Chinese torture of procedure on you, order you about with less grace than a cur, and threaten you with "consequences," and when you can't take it anymore, then *you* are the one to be blamed, fined, and humiliated. It's the world upside-down. I always thought that as citizens, we ought to have the right to carry a riding crop and to use it at will upon rude civil servants. As ever Churchill said it best when he spoke of civil servants who "are no longer civil and who no longer serve." Why do we take it? We pay the bill, damn it!

Such reflections readily take us to consider our police. Now it's true that save for a blessed moment in English history, the cops have not been paragons of good grace. But they were civil. Now, they are anything but, with due apologies to the few who are. They won't disagree with my judgment. Some malady struck our—I speak of the Western democracies—police over the course of the last twenty years, or a shade more perhaps. They have come to see themselves as a paramilitary force, and they love to play soldier. Who knows, maybe it was the *Rambo* effect, the films exciting immature minds. We now systematically attract poorly adjusted young people—hostile, angry, vengeful—to our police forces. They get dressed up as SWAT types and unsmilingly swagger around our towns and countryside looking like Mussolinis in a Monty Python skit—funny, but not when you have to deal with them. They have all but given up protecting us from true criminals—it is beyond them apparently—so they devote themselves to providing the state with additional revenues, hassling us, and tracking down easy marks who do not jeopardize any of their corrupt arrangements or their donut vagrancy. Their chiefs are promoted from their pool, and somehow the supposed civilian supervision doesn't exist. All the commissioners and the police commissions ever do is to congratulate these aggressive oafs on "their service." Service, my ass. We could do it better ourselves, as many communities once did.

This new police, confronted with complex and slightly menacing situations, such as a citizen asking for directions, are likely—even if they grudgingly condescend to assist—to let you know that you've been a bother. What do they think they are for? Have you ever been stopped for minor speeding, the "for revenue" violation rather than the reckless one? The "trooper" shows up at your car window having sauntered over à la John Wayne and puffs himself up, striking a baritone, "License and registration!" Whatever happened to "Good morning, afternoon, evening, sir/ma'am"? What happened to lending a sense of decency to one's information and request as, "I think you were going a little fast. May I have your license and registration please?" What are they afraid of? That if they say please, their balls will fall off? What we have in our modern cops—yeah, the girls, too, in some bizarre miscarriage of biology—is in fact some testicles connected to a bit of cerebral cortex and wrapped in muscle ... or flab. They can no longer look or behave as human beings. It's them against us. Have you ever seen one of their funerals? It's Roman emperor stuff; a cast of thousands; streets closed off—don't ask about a parade permit: there isn't any; and "they" are the law—and a budget to make Spielberg faint. Do we begrudge them honoring one of their colleagues? Not for a minute! We begrudge their mounting these ridiculous in-your-face circuses to which fellow gladiators come from afar—individuals who never remotely knew the deceased. Who pays for all this? Guess.

What about the locking elbows instinct these thugs have? Let any among them do the most horrible of things, and the penetration of their ring—their omertà—will still require an act by the attorney general, the legislature, or a yet higher power. The premise is that "they can do no wrong." This has led to the vastly more dangerous understanding that they are the law. They are not. And the law is not what they say; it's what the law says. But now cops routinely invent law to suit themselves, their simple souls suborned by fawning officials calling them heroes.

Heroes. Give me a break, or at least a dictionary: *1. In mythology or legend a man, often born of one mortal and one divine parent, who is endowed with great courage and strength, celebrated for his bold exploits, and favored by the gods. 2. Any man noted for feats of courage or nobility of purpose; especially one who has risked or sacrificed his life.* Recognize your local state trooper there? Maybe not. What if they had haircuts that didn't give them the astonished boot-camp look? What if they doffed their hats? What if they weren't dressed up in paramilitary uniforms? What if they were taught to say please and thank you? You never know, they might even be given smiling lessons. Wouldn't that make life better, and, not incidentally, their work more effective? Our police today, throughout the Western democracies, are too often self-important bullies who are poorly trained, unsupervised, and set out among us with a compulsive surliness. From the standpoint of good policing, which entirely depends upon the community, this aggressive sourness is the most ineffective of choices. With 90 percent or more of the citizenry being generally law-abiding, the best concept of public order is that in which the community maintains order with the occasional assistance of an officer they have hired for the purpose. What we as law-abiding citizens today feel is that we are the prey—surely because we're easy marks, and the criminals are left to run wild. Why do we put up with it?

In the UK, a vast horde of busybodies have put their noses into every facet of private life, urged on, it would seem, by some malignant chromosome that wants safety above all. To be fair, this has afflicted Americans, too, but the heights it has attained in the UK are agoraphobic. Moreover, attached to each new regulation is the ever-present admonition that "Abusive behavior will not be tolerated." No one ever thought to consider the systematic abuse wrought upon the population by these busybodies: the wasted time, the humiliation, the frustration, and the destruction of life's happiness. We consider it better, in order to preserve one immigrant from one rude remark—because that is what a racial slur is, a rude remark—to inconvenience an entire population, to constrain it in its speech, and to remove it from any sense of liberty.

I remember reading the novelist Saul Bellow's account of growing up in south Chicago. "It was pretty rough," he explained, "but not unfriendly for all that. We called each other names—kike, jig, spic, wop—but we didn't really mean anything by it. We got along. We played stick ball in the street together. Now, the least off-color word gives offense. The communities are on edge. There's no freedom left. We were better off then, in my old neighborhood, freer and friendlier."

The rudeness has brought with it a terribly self-centered preciousness. Having neither breeding nor manners, the iPod generation thinks it is owed everything and does not have to give anything in exchange. Kings and queens say thank you to their servants, but these kids seem unable to find the words. Perhaps they don't know them. I don't mean that they have not heard them; I mean that they don't understand their use. The fly on the wall in the restaurants in which they congregate is privy to bizarre dialogues with the waiters, in which the waiter is alternately addressed as a lord and a serf; to table manners it is best not to see, a fast-backward to Elizabethan dining entirely devoid of the redeeming lustiness; to electronically interrupted dialogue between themselves at often extraordinary volumes, as though they were the only party in the room; and—as we've already commented upon—to every "me" fashion now current, with everything being about my comfort, and yours be damned. How can such behavior not be carried into their professional lives?

Everyone has suffered a tale as this, wherein, after having gone through all the waits, delays, and tribulations that are today accepted in the calling of an airline, one has managed to get a live human voice. It has been twenty minutes of aggravation, but finally the ticket will be changed. Wrong. The agent decides he doesn't care for *your* irritation, and after the shit his airline has just put you through, he says to you: "I don't like your attitude. I'm going to hang up." Click. You have no choice about what happens then to your blood pressure, no choice about what you're going to do to get the ticket changed, no choice about how you might get through to someone who would in fact act as though *you* were the customer—and maybe someone who would horsewhip the agent who cut you off. No one ever had the small consideration to provide an ombudsman, a path for the resolution of special problems. It is entirely rude. It invites retaliation. Thus do we lose our civility.

If you ever have a case of multiple fraudulent charges on your credit card, you will be in for a treat. Here is what happens. First, there is a suggestion that maybe you're the tricky bugger—you feel yourself placed basically on a par with the crooked merchant—and you are told that "if after investigation what you have said can be confirmed, then ..." Second, you will be sent an affidavit to complete, requiring much information, to affirm your position that the charge is fraudulent. Note that the word charge is singular. That's right, there is no mechanism to group fraudulent charges made by a single merchant, and you will be obliged to complete an affidavit for each and every charge. Are there fourteen? There are. Tough. Do you think they can then post the fourteen affidavits and treat these together, the pattern being self-evident even to a dim first-year bookkeeper? Not at all. They will be considered individually. This is madness, say you, give me a supervisor. "I'm sorry, but we don't have access to a supervisor." It goes on and on. I learned from one not unkind soul, who did understand but could not change the policy to serve me decently, that—and this is pure genius—she worked somewhere in Minnesota, and her "supervisor" worked on the East Coast, but she had no way to communicate with her supervisor. The offender must be named: Citigroup.

Not only did this procedure vastly inconvenience me for a fraud committed by a merchant, taking up many hours of my time, but it also lost Citigroup many hours. An intelligent person authorized to do the right thing would have had the business done in ten minutes ... and a satisfied customer. No one cares. The machine is the thing; the program, the policy, the god of iron procedure must be served. We tend to think of these incidents as massively frustrating, of course, but they are something more basic than that: just rude—a mirror, surely, of those behind the mechanism. Such institutionalized rudeness, greatly facilitated and perhaps unintentionally encouraged by our IT world, is universal today, a consequence of the increasing isolation between us. At first the goal seemed only functional, to allow automation to handle what it could; now the goal seems to have extended well beyond that, with systems actually designed to *prevent* any human contact. We could see this as the ultimate democratization of society, whereby everybody gets the same contempt and short shrift once reserved for the most wretched among us. Today, unless one commands extreme wealth, one will suffer inconvenience democratically. It might have been more thoughtful to democratize privilege.

There is no single explanation for this tide of bad manners. IT is surely not the lone culprit. Probably a sociologist could point to the breaking down of class barriers that began in the nineteenth century and to which WWII brought a certain finality, those having suffered together and survived together less willing than their parents to maintain distinctions between themselves. Unfortunately society tends to function according to the economic law holding that the bad money drives out the good, with the rougher habit of speech and comportment usurping the more refined.

Another restraint was lost with the feminist movement, which willed that females should be exposed equally with males to coarseness.

Women civilize: when we make them men, we lose civilization. There is nothing now that cannot be spoken in the presence of females. To some it is a triumph, to others a shame, but perhaps all could agree that it has been an agent of change in our manners.

Before the advent of our click-and-acknowledge technology we were compelled to maintain some human contact.

Living in the country as I do, I have perceived one striking change in our habits that I feel says it all. Anyone older than forty can recall that it was obligatory, when driving along a wooded lane, upon encountering a pedestrian, for driver and pedestrian to acknowledge each other. It made no difference that the two were strangers: still they would exchange a small wave, a nod, a gesture, and always eye contact. Now it's all the opposite. Eye contact is studiously avoided, and just forget the wave. When we walk in the street in a city, it is the same: a feeling of navigating countercurrent to a school of alien fish, their eyes unemotional and diverted.

In public spaces, as the Underground in London, it goes a level further, the ambulatory cyberhuman walking into the station already isolated by the music pumped into him through his iPod earphones, his gaze upon the ground as one of those new self-steering vacs, his person encapsulated. His eyes will only ever meet yours furtively, and then without recognition for a fellow human, only to be immediately averted to the more comfortable view of a stainless steel fascia or an empty glass pane that reflects only silent fluorescent ghosts. It was never polite to stare, but it was as impolite to ignore; one acknowledged another's presence. Everyone knew how to do that agreeably without suggesting a need for further contact. It made a train ride more pleasant, not feeling as though one wore a "pedophile" sign on oneself.

It seems that in our new world, women consider all men rapists, mothers fear for their infants, teenagers are assumed to mean trouble (that has some historical justification), and the races—in our multiracial world—suspect each other more than ever while pretending not to. I believe that in the antebellum South, a white lady would have visually acknowledged a black slave; today, no one exists for another, a form of dehumanization that may prove more difficult to correct than the breaking of fetters.

Civilization—and, not insignificantly, our dignity and liberty—depend upon human interaction. A text message is only marginally human. It is absolutely useful in lieu of a footman sent to give information, but absolutely futile for the expression of any emotion. The modern tendency in business is unemotional—not in the older sense of hard-nosed—but in a newer way, devoid of emotion. It is thought to be efficient, and therefore clever, a form of techno-macho espoused by male and female alike—the shorter the communication, the better.

Yet, successful relationships are built upon emotion. Shackleton did not secure the devotion and complete confidence of his men by sending them text messages. A competent physician understands that often an illness is as an iceberg: the visible and smaller part physical, and the hidden major part emotional. In fact, the failure to understand this truth is a huge problem with our new generation of techno-docs who stare into their laptops without ever seeing—really seeing—their patients. They inspire no confidence. And for most ills, it is confidence that cures. At the technological extremity, our medicine is sci-fi stuff, but for most of what ails us, the understanding and reassurance that once healed no longer exist.

I return to human communication as the basis for society, civility, dignity, and liberty. Is not in fact a society of liberty one civilly construed and offering its members individual respect and dignity? It might not be the entire pie, but it counts most of the slices.

Examples of government rudeness to its citizens are so common and habitual that the lack of manners has become an expectation: "What did you expect? It's the government." Well, no. Actually what I expect is that the government behaves as *my servant*. It was established by us in free Congress for the very purpose. It is paid for by us. The sleepy-angry bureaucrat who just snarled at you is on your payroll. An example *sans pareil*, once we get beyond the motor vehicle bureau (a hell Dante never imagined), is the immigration service. Pick a country, any country. These functionaries are all pared from the same bad turnip.

Their first object is to let you know that you disinterest them. You weary them. But for your inconvenient arrival, they could be yukking it up in the coffee room, texting their girlfriends, or watching the game. *You,* you sniveling little worm, had to come along and break into *their* day. They have cultivated a glazed-eye sneer for this purpose, a sneer that looks beyond you. You don't merit existence. Their second purpose is to let you know that they know you're hiding something. You wrote on the form—in reply to a question of entirely uncertain legality—that you'd visited France and Italy? Yeah, sure. You also went to Spain, but you're hiding it, you worthless little coward. Anyway, real Americans don't travel abroad, don't even have passports. You travel? Hmm, that's suspicious. Last, they want you to understand the *power* in their hands. They can make your next hour miserable. With these three in hand—and understanding how greatly we inconvenience them by being—they grunt and grimace and bark. Did you forget to sign one of the forms? It's thrown across the desk at you. "Sign here!" An angry finger indicates where. You feel the officer's approach is really not right for a civil servant. You suggest—politely, deferentially, humbly, that he might say "please." Ha! Now you've prodded the beast. The look, first of dumb incomprehension and then of anger—sort of as a primitive animal whose nervous system only slowly communicates pain from hindquarters to brain—tells you that now you've really crossed the line. You see two emotions battling within the creature, one its inbred indolence and the other its rising ire. Which will win has more to do with the closeness of the game it wants to get back to than any consideration for you.

Why do we take it? Are we not free citizens of allegedly free countries? Are these individuals not *our* civil servants? Do we not tax ourselves to pay them? And what do the people at the top of these pyramids of functionaries not understand? (*Solution: the commissioner ought to be made to travel internationally ten times per month, anonymously to the immigration service, entering the United States alternately via New York or Los Angeles. If he still doesn't get it, make him enter on a foreign passport. Welcome to the United States!*) But this is old hat, as old as man. Government functionaries perfected the twin virtues of disdain and sloth so long ago that it's now been found as a mutation in their DNA. These are *isolated* people, they and we, and now we're doing it between ourselves.

When we break down communication between human beings, we break down families. When we break down families, we oblige a replacement, for so we are made. The surrogate is a dangerous one that always consumes dignity and liberty: the state.

We are forgetting that we are not machines; that we are complex; that our balance is delicate; that in denying what is natural we upset our and society's equilibrium. Speak of tipping points, here is a tipping point! Once again we are compelled by history to be ever optimistic and pessimistic. Things change. Can they change soon, please?

A final thought is this: we shall have to better learn to live with IT. If we think in analogies, we can find some appropriate ones. In business it was once considered necessary to efficiency to reserve times in one's schedule for specific purposes—in fact to *avoid* interruptions. We understood that to complete a task well, one needed concentration and reflection. A manager in the era of written correspondence normally kept a time each morning—no interruptions allowed—to read and answer the mail. Then he could go on to either such technical tasks as he might have had—by closing the door to concentrate—or to the major part of any manager's job, to see and to speak with colleagues and subordinates. Now we see managers who fancy themselves actors in some Bond movie, remote and unseen beings exercising power from some aerie, giving instructions by electronic code. It's no good. The all-day all-night, minute-by-minute communication robs us of the *major part* of our working time and of all of our concentration. In due course the market will recognize this. Solutions remain to be found, but they do not seem inscrutably obscure: wean the kids of the video-game habit (time to grow up, in effect); order one's working day as of old, with reserved times for specific things; and establish the habit of leaving the electronic gadgets in one place. We didn't walk around the office carrying typewriters.

In private life we'll need to do much the same. One view is that the Internet has only taken the place TV had, as TV took the place books had. Some of this is true. There is nothing against reading a book on a screen rather than on paper. Some is not true, replacing moments of calm—in the best of cases, introspection and instruction—with agitated, meaningless activity: checking, checking, checking, all empty space. Did you used to run out to your mailbox thirty times per hour? The use of tools is one of man's distinguishing characteristics, not the tools' use of men. Time for the Reset button, methinks.

It would be an omission not to comment upon the upbringing most parents are giving their kids these days. Dr. Spock has much to answer for. He did. In his later years he had at least the honesty to reflect, "When I see the generation of kids my counsel has raised, I have to think I was wrong." Thank you, Doctor. Now, what do you suggest we do with the brats? They grow up to become thugs—some intellectually, some physically, some both. And they still pick their noses, fail to cover their coughs, wear baseball caps to dinner, do not rise when a lady enters the room and belch with Elizabethan abandon. For one and all, therefore, I give this contribution freely and from the goodness of my heart: *It is not true that it benefits children to be raised without discipline.* And it sure as hell makes life miserable for the rest of us. P.S.: It also helps if they can be made to understand that complete sentences have communicative value.

Chapter 9
Rights and Privacy in the IT Age

A concern that may prove liberty's greatest challenge, encompassing all of the fears which gave us a Bill of Rights and the Rights of Man, is privacy. Liberty is a lily pad. Privacy is the pond. We will not have the one without the other. Tyrants are by nature and purpose hostile to privacy. The physical and moral zone defined by privacy is one upon which the tyrant cannot enter. Thus his tyranny is incomplete. So a measure of liberty exists. The more there is privacy, the more there is liberty. Now government—the tyrant—and the people who in their primitive fear turn to it for succor, conspire to destroy privacy. IT is the handmaid. The combination of these into a triad made sinister by the conjuncture in time and place of a warlord, a fearful people, and electronic shackles may prove *fatal* to liberty.

We evoked in Chapter 1 the understanding that liberty is a fragile thing, assuredly not any kind of natural state for man. Liberty is always under assault by the stationary bandit, the government, but may be safeguarded for a time by a vigilant people and a constitutional understanding that *reserves* vital rights for the people. The moment the stationary bandit can know all, can have eyes and ears everywhere, liberty dies. A very dangerous notion heard in the post-9/11 years is the bleat of the fearful citizen who declares, not without sanctimony, "If you have done nothing wrong, you shouldn't have anything to worry

126

about ... I don't mind if the government looks into my private affairs to keep me safe ... I've nothing to hide." This is false. All of us have something to hide. This has been the sharp knife wielded by tyrants for all time. Everyone in Stalin's purges was legally charged with a crime. *Everyone.* The assumption of good faith, where it concerns a government, is an illusion of the naive. They shall be sheep to slaughter.

The good faith of government does not exist. We have only to look at the recent past in the Western democracies, most notably in the United States in the years after 2001, to see how government did ask for and receive extraordinary unconstitutional powers—yes, by some kind of emergency, thus securing cowed assent—promising us that these would be used solely for the purpose of combating terrorism. Too many bought the deal.

There were two things wrong: a government promise is meaningless, and terrorism is such a vague notion that it can be—and now has been—applied to everything and anything. That's precisely what Stalin did with "sabotage." Anyone could be a saboteur, and many died for it but sabotaged nothing. It was an invention. The Israelis, clever and pragmatic always, instantly understood the Bush administration's fixation with terrorism and wasted no time converting Palestinian revolutionaries into so-called terrorists. Given the inclination of the Bush crowd to swallow whatever old fish the Israelis threw at them, urged on by Israel's own in the administration, they gulped this one whole. If the Palestinians are terrorists, George Washington was a terrorist. It is all a matter of perspective and inclination.

Our not-very-bright but ever opportunistic police were not so dim that they didn't want terrorists of their very own, and thus the tag was stapled onto common criminals who were, well, common criminals. Counterterrorism was in vogue, the flavor of the day. That's where the money was. Did you want a patrol boat for an isolated New England lake, simply because the next town over had been so silly as to procure one? Terrorism. That was the password. It would get you anything. You just never know when militant trout will rise up. They had a field day (the cops, not the trout). In the Soviet Union, those who were not in the government's favor were "counter-revolutionaries." In the United States of 2009, they were "terrorists."

Who believes that we will ever regain the rights we lost in the last decade? Can we point to a government that ever kept its word? If we want those rights back, rights that remain constitutionally ours, we shall have to fight for them. Have we the backbone? Our rah-rah-foreign-wars types are a raucous and swaggering bunch, but I very much doubt they have the guts for the fight, or the wit to understand what has been lost. Liberty is too delicate a flower for them. They prefer what they have baptized FREEDOM in capital letters, proclaimed with puffed-out chests and tears in their eyes. Look once at the old black-and-white photos of Adolf Hitler driving through crowds in Germany before the war: flags and flags and flags, puffed out chests, arms raised in happy obedient salute to the new god, tears in every eye. It's only a thin line. A very thin line.

What rights did we lose? They have one common thread: privacy. The government wants to know everything about us. What we say. Whom we see. What we write. What we think, or what others—informers—think we think. It isn't a welcoming perspective. We have followed a false path.

The ever burgeoning IT of the world is the tool. There is nothing electronic that cannot be accessed, stored, and processed. The accessing of it, which was once illegal, which once required a very specific court order, now comes under blanket powers. No protection remains. A right unprotected is a right lost. Now the government wants to make it easy for itself; electronic data must be kept by those through whose servers it passes. New cell phones must show GPS coordinates. You can run, but you can't hide. All of your records can be obtained by the government with facility under sweeping emergency powers. Your calls and e-mail are monitored by nightmarish Big Brother technology.

And we so lost our courage that we said not a word; in fact we were complicit and clanged the grate shut upon ourselves. What kind of Americans have we become? The kids today don't even grow up knowing about the sanctity of the mail, the absolute privacy we relied upon only a generation ago. How comes it that e-mail doesn't enjoy the same protection? It isn't the form of the mail … it's the principle, isn't it? As in everything else, the government seizes a power and then enlarges it. Several decades ago the government established the RICO act, ostensibly to pursue organized crime. It didn't take a year before prosecutors began to wield it against citizens who were not even remotely criminals; they used it the way Stalin's prosecutor Vizinshky used the charge of sabotage, in the pursuit of vicious political prosecutions. Eavesdropping used to require a very specific court order. Now, without a whimper, we assume we are listened to. For international calls, the government has used a twisted logic and America's longtime isolationist streak to make it seem entirely right that it listens. After all, honest, loyal citizens don't make international calls, do they? They don't even know anyone foreign.

Is it our public business that a man in Oregon has a girlfriend in Turkey? That a woman thinks her stepsister should inherit less? That a company wants to structure an alliance with another to surprise a market? That a patient wishes to consult his doctor regarding a condition embarrassing to himself? That an individual wants to buy a house anonymously? That a wife desires to travel without it being known? That a teacher thinks a pupil needs private advice? That a couple judges it prudent to place some funds beyond potential future creditors? All no! It is none of our business! Moreover, our whole body of law forbids us to read some putative future criminal intent into a citizen's private affairs. We need to keep—now more to the point, to restore—one of the foundation stones of our liberty: *innocent until proven guilty.*

We used to have some fairly well-respected laws against entrapment. They're gone. Entrapment is a particularly vile tactic of police forces with too much time on their hands. They seek to lure citizens into committing crimes. It's a do-it-yourself crime-and-arrest game. The vice squad sends out a policewoman to solicit, hoping to find a taker. Then—bingo—humiliation and arrest. The bunko crew sets up a poker game, gets the word around, and then arrests the participants. Officers with much malice and little decency set up pornographic sites to inveigle the unsuspecting.

These are manufactured crimes. There may be, with a careful process of court approval in each and every individual case, the rare place for a sting. A court could only approve a sting directed at a person of known criminality, with good and sound evidence in hand. What we are dealing with are unqualified fishing expeditions wherein we are all potential targets, the practice hostile to liberty and inadmissible to a society that wants itself free. It diverts the police from their duty, and it supports a gaming culture whereby the officers involved challenge themselves to find ever more creative ways to entrap.

Why not remove the No Parking signs from a no-parking zone and then slap fines on those who park there? That would be fun. You think I am exaggerating. Yet, it's only one step from what the police do in some states: driving too fast on the highway, without emergency, and then arresting motorists following them at like speed. It is plain-as-day entrapment. We just take it. Or constructing artificial speed limit zones—a sudden 300-yard 30 mph section, without visible reason, bracketed between 50 mph stretches. Easy. That'll yield plenty of revenue, every time. Is it honest? Does it engender respect for the law? Why do we take it? It happens all of the time, everywhere.

In the UK they discovered that speed cameras can be in more places at once than human officers, greatly multiplying revenues—sums that run into the hundreds of millions of pounds. In many of these locations, there's no serious pretense that the camera combats risk. Everyone understands that. It's about revenue. Why do the Brits take it? The Germans are more organized and more technical, so they have cameras controlling a far greater range of offenses—distance between vehicles, for example—so that driving in Germany has become a full-time video game with hazards—the cameras—jumping out at you left and right. Do we think this makes driving safer? We build our societies into an understanding that all are guilty; it is just a matter of catching them. Once we go down that path, the breath of totalitarianism is upon us. Are we not better off morally and economically to suppose our citizens innocent until proven guilty? Once our societies come to be the law versus citizens, liberty ceases to exist. Do not all of these violations derive from breaches of privacy?

Privacy is the right a man has to himself, to his own person. The founders of the American republic could never have imagined that to which we have come, could not have conceived of the present violation of our lives by the state. Had they considered it a risk, however remote, Article 4 of the Bill of Rights would have greatly elaborated its constraints upon government intrusion. One of the points we shall consider in this chapter will be the addition of an article to be added to the Constitution—a specific privacy amendment. The difficulty in moving the amendment will be the busybodies who now buzz for safety at all costs with the insistence of mosquitoes in spring.

There are among us—for social matters, generally the liberals, and for security matters, generally the new type of conservatives—busybodies. Both—for our own good, they assure us—want to dictate to us what we must do, and both conclude that as we aren't in their eyes fit adults, the state must do for us. I was careful in the instance of conservatives to specify the new type, the flag-and-war-and-country gang, who have nothing in common with what a conservative used to be in American politics: a proponent of small government and free markets, a defender of constitutional rights, in effect a libertarian. As in many of our Western democracies the debate over the just size of government is no longer on. Big government corrupted everyone. Now the entire political battle is over whom will wear the crown, the sort of thing that was the soup of the day in the age of kings and nobles. No one disputed the monarchy, only the monarch.

The busybodies are going to do us good, whether we want it or not. And when we oppose their intrusions into our lives, they become accusatory and ever ready to vilify. They always have some PhD to hand as an expert witness. Thus we must learn from some goateed bachelor shrink how children must be raised, disregarding the mother who has raised three kids. We must obey the rules for the placement of a ladder set by a functionary, giving no credence to the roofer for whom working with ladders has been a livelihood. We must fish according to the dictates of some timid landlubber, dismissing the knowledge of captain and crew. Perhaps it is the price we pay for having channeled so many of modest intellect away from trades, where they might have been productive, to desk work for which they are manifestly unsuited.

Whatever the cause, the result is a vast web—think of a large and tangled ball of string—of petty and unfathomable regulations governing everything we do—and now, all too often, what we say. Did you compliment your female sales director on a pretty scarf? Inappropriate! You might have to resign. Did you kick a stray ball back to a child in a public park? Hmm. If you're not already a pedophile, you probably have the inclination. We'll be watching you. Did you let off with some coarse language when a machine operator broke—for the third time—a vital machine? Intimidating conduct. The operator has rights. You are abusive. No, we don't care that the breakdown put half a dozen employees out of work for a week. That's your problem. What we care about is abusive you. These busybodies, private and public, are people of no productive inclination in life. Of course they have always existed, but never so many as now. Life was harder, getting a square meal each day a struggle, and there just wasn't the time for this sort of self-indulgence. That is what it is: vain self-indulgence, whereby individuals inclined to reproach the world doing what they cannot do make a profession of intruding upon those who can. There is a place for the kindergarten teacher … in the kindergarten.

Some of this goes back to the "mom rules/dad rules" dichotomy we already examined. We can say what we want, but nature has the last word; men and women do not—by their natures—have the same perspective on things. When, as in the Western democracies, women come to claim their imminently justifiable rights, society must find a new equilibrium. We have overshot the mark. Equal pay for equal work seems an undeniable right, extending to all labor. That a daughter should have every opportunity open to a son seems just. These are less, from a standpoint of liberty in the abstract, a matter of granting rights; they are a matter of not denying rights. Once we begin to deny rights, there is no end to it. On the other hand this does not mean that all roles are as well suited to one sex as to the other. When we pretend that our notion of roles is only cultural, we have an understanding that is untrue. I don't propose to enter into a polemic upon the subject, and the reader will either understand what I say by common experience, or not. The result, objectively speaking, is that women have brought a great deal more of themselves into the ordering of public life than previously, for better and worse, just as men always brought themselves into it, for better and worse. The weakness in our modern understanding is that "better and worse" is held true for men, but as regards women, we are only allowed to consider the better. The worse, we are told, doesn't exist—and it's only muddleheaded, sexist, or criminal of us to think it. Well, it ain't so.

By the introduction of women into public life, we have gotten, for example, one very feminine manner of thought, the notion that "something must be done," never mind that it is half-baked and never mind the consequences. Don't you see? Something must be done! Well, it isn't true in many cases that something must be done, and when it is done under such circumstances, it usually is an assault on our rights and our privacy, not to mention common sense. The women, whose feminist movement went from the serious to the absurd—we can perhaps be forgiven recalling those libbers who wanted the right to use urinals— became a very strong movement with a profound effect upon society. Most men in the Western democracies were affected. Some—a faction of the timid, I would suggest with tongue in cheek—came to espouse the whole mantra and converted themselves into virtual women. Others, adept at seeing how the wind blows, very cynically decided that a port tack would be better for a time. Even the hardiest took note, the clever taking the good of the movement and minimizing the bad, and so the equilibrium of society tilted to a new axis. It's the busybodies and the cynics we must be concerned for. All dictators are cynics, and cynicism is the hallmark of the hierarchy of authoritarianism that exists under any dictator. The busybodies are their tools. The game is about power. We are the pawns.

Yes, but weren't we speaking about privacy? We are. Intrusion into our lives is not ordered from on high. It has a cause. The cause is the conjuncture at one time of overlarge government and a significant number of people who, through the prosperity brought by free markets, have the leisure to indulge their worst instinct—to intrude upon their fellows—rather than having to win their daily bread. We are the victims. Any historian would make the comment that this conjuncture—large government and general prosperity—was never a precondition to intrusive government. Correct. Intrusiveness obtains in two circumstances, the first we have limned here above, and the second is the case of a tyranny over an impoverished realm, wherein the tyrant bankrupts the land to keep his power, acting through an insufferable hierarchy of minions. Think of Duvalier's Haiti, the late Ottoman Empire, the Chinese and Soviet communist empires. We are not there yet, but viewed from the perspective of history, the risk of eventual impoverishment through economic paralysis is now greater for the Western democracies than it was in more liberal times. Gulliver can only survive so many Lilliputians.

Everything has a price, moral or economic—often both. We cannot give without taking away. We cannot take without loss. This was my concern when I spoke here above about the need some feel to "do something," never mind the consequences; they refuse to even try to imagine these.

Let us take for an example the 2009 debate in the United States regarding health care. Is there a problem? Yes. Most agree. What is the problem? Most don't agree. Each has his own view. Is there some common ground? Yes. Somehow we know we must address the uninsured, and most of us understand that our health care, taken as a whole, has become far too expensive. How do we fix the problem? Ah, there is the rub. First, it isn't obvious. Second, experience with government programs and requirements suggests extreme caution: four out of five government actions—maybe it's more—go wrong through *unintended consequences*. This is the trap that lurks for all who would do good without first asking two questions: Have I the right, the constitutional and moral right, to do this act that I define as good but that another may not? And have I fully weighed the consequences?

In the 1960s, a forceful president, Lyndon Johnson, brought his vision to the nation in the form of the Great Society. A fan would say it brought much humanity to America by the support it gave to a grab-bag class (then defined as the underprivileged), whereas a critic would argue that it was the greatest vote-buying exercise in our history. The argument raged. After a generation a common ground was found nonetheless between fan and critic: the program had had serious moral and economic consequences for millions of citizens, locking them into a prison of public assistance and despair, virtually assuring that their children would follow in their footsteps. Those with cooler heads had argued this very point as the Great Society was mooted, but had found themselves lumped with those whose morality instructed them to give no help. There is an ocean of difference between not wishing to give help for the principle of the thing and not giving help because one can see that it will do harm. Today the nation, as do all the Western democracies, carries the huge burden of these programs and finds itself with as many or more of the underprivileged as it ever had. We created a permanent burden, without economic utility and to the detriment of human dignity, while robbing the majority.

These are the great issues of the day. The Federalists anticipated them and deliberately sought to construct a government of checks and balances, of due process, and of laborious action. They were skeptical that man could keep his liberty. They did as good a job crafting the institutions as might have been asked. They didn't give sufficient weight to the nature of man to desire power, and of a society to be cowed by it.

This returns us to the matter of privacy. Without violating privacy, a government is greatly constrained in its violation of liberty. The breach of privacy is the necessary tool for tyranny. IT makes this tool pervasive, invasive, and insidious.

We will be obliged to think deeply upon the subject of privacy. Failing that, we won't have to think much at all. A prisoner in a cell can dream, but he doesn't need to think.

Chapter 10
Taxes, Abuse, and Collapse

Without private property, liberty does not exist. The sole source of income in an economy is the labor of the individual. The art of the stationary bandit—the government—is to make citizens believe that neither of these is true and thus—as a nineteenth-century British prime minister said—to pluck the goose with the least amount of hissing.

Tax policy in the Western democracies today is one of the greatest engines of societal destabilization, a monstrous pyramid scheme that steals from the productive to give to the unproductive in the pursuit of political power. The extent to which the citizen is abused is deliberately concealed by the fractionalization of taxes, charges, fees, mandates, and inflation—a grand sleight of hand—in order to keep citizens in the belief that they inhabit "free" countries; they are in fact no more than half free … and half slave. This in another context did not strike a prior generation of Americans as tenable, and it became one of the causes of the Civil War. It is no more tenable in the current context, even as the circumstances are different. It is not a peculiarly American problem; the other Western democracies are as much affected.

What is a slave? A slave, in our modern understanding, is a man in chains, bought and sold at will, as property, harshly punishable at his owner's whim. We have always recognized other forms of bondage that exist on a continuum, at one extreme that unhappy being corresponding to the image we have conjured above, at the other what we might call a free man, and between these a bondage or a freedom of degrees. Was a serf a slave? In many respects, yes. An indentured servant? For a time. An eighteenth-century domestic servant? A twenty-first-century maid in Saudi Arabia? No, perhaps not slaves in some respects, but otherwise little freer than slaves. A tenant farmer? A sharecropper? No, but we get the point. A modern "wage slave"? No, surely not, but we understand the metaphor. So what is, in the current fashion of speech, the tipping point?

A slave needs to meet several tests for us to call him one. I propose the following. First, he must be the property by law of another. Second, he is bound to give all or most of his labor, without remuneration save bed and board, to his owner. Third, his physical locality is dictated by the wish of his owner. Fourth, his owner may dispose of him more or less as he sees fit.

If we can agree upon these conditions of slavery, then clearly the classic Western image of the Egyptian slave of antiquity defines a state of unmitigated slavery. The same condition might have been found in much of the ancient world. Let us remember that society was then so constructed that the great majority of our own distant ancestors were slaves, largely meeting the four tests here above.

Now let us consider a serf. The word is different, but most of the conditions of slavery are met. There wasn't much to choose from between being a slave and a serf. The distinctions were no more than nuances. We have the idea that a serf could have some sort of a family life—indeed he could, remembering nonetheless that his lord had to approve his marriage and enjoyed the right to deflower his bride—and that he might look to dying in the village of his birth. Small distinctions.

What about a citizen in the communist regimes of the twentieth century? On paper he was a free man; in practice, hardly. If we doubt, let us look again at the tests. Property of another? Not as such, but he could be in most respects treated as property. Labor owed to a master? To the extent that he was not free to sell his labor at a fair market value, and that the state—the master—took the greater part of his labor for itself and left him with the bare necessity, akin to room and board, we would have to say yes, his labor was owed to another. Physical locality dictated by the master? Yes. Citizens were not free to move without state approval. Finally, could the state dispose of its citizens and whatever small effects they considered theirs as it saw fit? Yes, undoubtedly, and it did. Conclusion: it is only by a political sentiment that impelled those in the West to try to see communism as benign and progressive that we did not—and still, to our shame, do not—recognize that the hundreds of millions of people who lived their lives under the red banner were for all practical purposes enslaved, if not precisely semantically slaves. If we could ask the millions who perished in the labor camps, they wouldn't mince their words. They would say it as it was: slavery.

It is not because a slave is humanely treated that he is not a slave. It has been often recorded that in the old South, some owners treated their slaves with humanity. We can know this without it changing our view that these poor men were slaves. The four conditions I have proposed do not include cruelty. Cruelty is a condition associated with slavery, but it is not necessary to it. We cannot use humanity to diminish slavery.

Slavery is largely an economic condition: that of being the property of another and of owing one's labor to another. The question is, how much is too much? What is the point too far? In our Western democracies, the state cannot dispose of us as property—with a notable and shocking exception in the United States, which "owns" us through a lifelong tax obligation wherever in the world we may live—but it can use us as property in some respects, military conscription being one. I grant that this isn't, for most of us, over the line, but neither is it self-evidently within bounds. On the question of labor, things are far less clear. If the critical point is 50 percent, we are more slave than not, for in almost all of the Western democracies the true tax take is above 50 percent.

We must return to Frédéric Bastiat. His brilliant insight was to understand that a tax on one is a tax on all. Let us take the instance of a medieval village. Over there is a church. Beyond, on the knoll, is the castle, the seat of the feudal lord. Between the church and the castle are the huts of the serfs, the shops of a few tradesmen, a forge, a farrier, a cooper, a mason. It is the lord's habit to spend a portion of his income locally each year, making various improvements to his castle or to the church, and sometimes even to the village. The harvest has just been taken in for the season. The weather was clement. It's a good harvest. The lord and the serfs will eat their fill this winter. But now come the king's men, a mounted troop. The king proposes to go to war—a foreign war for flag and glory. His army requires grain and his treasury gold. A third of the grain in the lord's granary—which is the village's granary— is seized, and one thousand ducats in gold are demanded. Who pays? Is it not the case that the entire village will now suffer for want of grain? And is it not likely that being one thousand ducats poorer, the lord will have to reduce, perhaps cancel, his works for the season? Who will suffer the loss? Is it not those villagers who were accustomed to perform the work? And these tradesmen seeing their incomes fail—with what might they then buy the small surplus the serfs are allowed to sell from their kitchen gardens? Thus the few coins the serfs had looked forward to will not be paid. The king, by taxing the lord, has in fact taxed the village. Economically it was inescapable. A tax on one is a tax on all. I have had this discussion many times with friends of more or less socialist persuasion. They are in no way stupid, yet they will never admit this argument. Is it because the argument is untrue, or is it because, should they ever admit the truth of the argument, their entire notion of a benign socialism would fall? I do not propose to review Bastiat's full thesis—one can consult it easily enough—but rather to use the force of what it implies as we inquire further into the modern understanding of the purpose of taxation, a system of control and acquisition of power that has little to do with the legitimate common revenue needs of our societies.

Who really pays? Once we comprehend the state's inability to excise a tax from one without affecting the others, of taking a spoonful of water from a bowl without dropping the water level, the reality becomes clear. In the United States we have some of the highest corporate taxes in the world—oddly enough, something the European social democracies got less wrong than we. The fact is, a corporation cannot pay a tax. It can collect a tax. It can remit a tax. But it cannot pay it. A corporation is an association of individuals, shareholders, and employees—customers, too—who come together because they see an advantage to themselves from a collective economic activity. In a simple example, a building corporation could be funded by three brothers, the shareholders; a dozen journeymen, the employees, working side by side with the shareholders; and a customer who gives them his confidence and his order for a new house. Let the government impose a 40 percent tax on the profit of this corporation. Who *pays* the tax? Is it not the customer who pays the money into the company from which the tax must perforce be taken? And the money being diverted from the company to government, can we agree that it is then no longer available to the employees or to the shareholders for wages or dividends? So, who has *paid* the tax? The only ones who could: the customer, the employees, and the shareholders. The company did no more than to collect and remit it.

Take a yet more basic example. A farm family and their hired hands dig an irrigation channel to draw water from a spring on their land. The government owns neighboring land, on which it places tenant farmers, and tells our farm family they will have to give a third of their water to the government, the representation being that groundwater belongs to the state. Moreover, our family will have to dig the channel conducting the water to government land. Thus our farm will now have a third less water and a one-third smaller crop. The farm family and the farmhands will have to make do with less, while giving of their labor to support a competitor. Did "the farm" give up the water, or did those who possessed the spring and who dug the channel give it up?

I will suggest to you that the 2009 bailout of GM by the government did exactly this to Ford; it took the money of Ford's shareholders and employees to fund a competitor. By what right? You work hard, you do well, and you are plundered. Isn't plunder what a highwayman does when he waylays a traveler? In the GM matter the plunder didn't stop at Ford; it extended to all American taxpayers. Wouldn't we have had a better deal by investing in Ford and letting Ford buy the depreciated assets of GM?

One last example: the fraud of social security. We have already said that government *fractionalizes* taxes to make them appear less than they are. So it is that many believe the social-security tax is paid "half-and-half"—by themselves and their employer. False! The entire social security tax is paid by the employee. How might it be otherwise? Is it not the value added provided by the employee's labor, which is taxed? The social-security tax is sleight of hand, a tax fractionalized to make it appear half of what it is! Moreover, it is a regressive tax, taking proportionately more from lower-wage earners than higher earners, as the tax has a cap above which it doesn't apply. For many lower-income earners, social security is the single largest tax they pay: in effect, over 15 percent of their incomes. To this one must add sales taxes, excise taxes, fees and registrations, income taxes, property taxes, capital gains taxes, dividends and interest taxes, fuel taxes, restaurant and lodging taxes, car rental taxes, airline ticket taxes, inheritance taxes ... well, you get the picture. And let us not overlook the darkest stealth tax of all—inflation—which undermines the value of our savings *and* causes us to pay real money on paper gains that are no more than an accounting fiction.

Lastly, fairly speaking we must also consider the time we are obliged to take and the accountants and lawyers we pay to sort out this unholy mess each year: a cost—thus a tax—imposed upon us by government through the unnatural and immoral complexity of the tax code. Add up all of these taxes, fees, and costs, and they don't leave any change from half or more of most of our incomes. Free ... or slave?

Let us return to the corporate tax, in the United States one of the highest in the world. Why does it matter to those of us who are not involved in corporations? After all, it's just the fat cats isn't it? Well, no. First, more of our employment depends on small corporations—less than fifty employees—than large. Second, most of us depend upon a corporation for our livelihoods. Third, the economy at large—which means all of us—depends upon the well-being of our corporations in the aggregate. These are rather robust reasons, taken as a whole, for us to care.

If we understand the economic verity that a corporation *cannot* pay a tax, but acts only as the collector and remitter of the tax (a tax in fact taken from us individually) and that it is only the government's sleight of hand making it appear as if the tax is paid by the corporation, we can become very concerned indeed. It is *our* money we're talking about! There is, however, something a corporation could do that would be of the greatest utility to us and to society: to save some money for a rainy day.

Politicians, who always want to take our money, want us to believe that "corporate money" has nothing to do with us; it's just about that fat cat who drives a fancy car. Well, it isn't. This goes back to Adam Smith's inspired understanding that others serve us not from munificence but from self-interest. When a shareholder of a corporation keeps earnings in the corporation, he has two choices regarding what to do with the money: he can invest it in the corporation, or he can hold it as a reserve. In the first case, he is—literally—investing in our livelihoods. Good! In the second case, he is providing for a rainy day, for the corporation and for us. Good! But now comes the stationary bandit—government— looking for his cut. And government wants such an amount that it in fact distorts the normal good application of the monies and undermines the entire capacity for a rainy-day reserve. As we have already examined, corporations do not earn anywhere near the popularly imagined profit. In fact it's rather a thin meal, taken as a whole. And then the government wants almost half of it! There isn't enough left to properly invest in the future of the corporation—our livelihood—and there certainly isn't enough left for a rainy day, which means, as it can only mean, that when the rainy day comes there will be hardship. There is no buffer. Moreover the amount the stationary bandit wants to seize is so great that the corporation will develop defensive strategies, which divert its purpose from earning money by its productive activity to protecting what money it earns; the economic integrity of purpose it ought to have is twisted and deformed. Everything is wrong in this, serving not the shareholders, not the employees, not society, and not even the government! It would have been far better, economically speaking, to tax the corporation not at all, in the same way a farmer will baby his best milk cow. Why burden the beast? She is his best producer! In this way productivity can be maximized, and the benefit is all to the farmer, the farmer's help, and the farmer's village. Ultimately such legitimate needs as the village may have will best be borne by lightly taxing its now prosperous residents, the *individuals* who are all the more prosperous for the farm's success.

As it is with villages, so it is with nations. Thus it is that Ibn Khaldūn wrote, "In the beginning of empires, taxes are low and the revenues of the state are high; at the end, taxes are high and revenues are low." We would be better off eliminating *all* taxes except the individual tax upon income, income being strictly defined as earnings created by the individual's value added labor. This is the source of all wealth. When we tax anything but this, we practice a deceit, seeking to hide the true level of taxation in order to prevent the goose hissing.

We should pass now to an understanding of the economic concept of *value added*. Value added is the foundation of all income, prosperity, and wealth. Without it, there is nothing. We begin with iron ore in the ground. It has no more than a potential value before it is mined, processed, and refined. At each one of these steps, there is value added: the miner who takes it from the ground enhances its potential, the processing that prepares it for refining makes it more valuable, and the refining of it for smelting yet again adds value. Each step entails the use of *ingenuity*—the intellectual labor at the root of all value added; *capital*—that investment in tools and infrastructure required by the activity; and *labor*—which realizes the work planned by ingenuity and enabled by capital. Note that capital is always and only the fruit of prior ingenuity and labor ... except in the case of the stationary bandit, who simply steals it.

Our refined ore proceeds to smelting, again adding value, and becomes an ingot from which metal may be drawn or formed. In an extreme case of value added, the ore may become a *katana,* a samurai sword, requiring untold hours of skilled labor to hone one of the world's most formidable blades. The final step in the value added manufacturing chain, that of the swordsmith, represents the single greatest addition of value, because it requires by far the most hours and the greatest skill. From ore in the ground to finished weapon there have been value-added steps, each manifestly making the product more valuable—economically speaking, *productive labor*—and making possible the payment of wages—*income*—and where such income shall exceed the laborer's daily needs, *savings,* which are the accumulation of capital. This interrelated notion of productive labor, value added, income, and wealth escapes many through want of clear understanding. Yet the peasant who toils and tills his own field understands it well enough.

On the understanding that we freely come together in communities to further our own interests—protection, security, promotion of prosperity through exchange—and that we judge it worth undertaking certain common expenditures as roads or ports for our common benefit, we come to the notion of a *contribution* from the labor of each toward a common purse. This is the legitimate basis of taxation. So long as such a contribution supports common needs and is truly done with the consent of those who are taxed, it remains relatively free of corruption. Let it begin to be used for wants in the place of needs, and it will immediately become corrupt, with individuals and factions vying for feed at the trough. Economically, the only honest, legitimate, and moral source of tax revenue is value added—that is individual income. It is individual labor or capital that produces value added. All other notions of income are made of the accountant's art, little more than hanging oranges on an apple tree and pretending that they grew thereupon.

The innocent will fear that should we adopt this understanding for our taxation it will abet the hiding of money from the eyes of the stationary bandit. On the contrary, it will not. Not only is it very nearly impossible to hide value added, but there would be no mechanism by which to do it. A man either earns or does not earn. If he earns, he contributes, and if he does not earn, he doesn't contribute. Another argument will be advanced that it somehow would be neither "fair"— the catchword of the demagogues—nor bearable to place the entire burden of taxation upon the individual. It would in fact be both, with an added benefit of immeasurable worth. First, it would be bearable, as a man would retain a greater part of his labor—what the Declaration of the Rights of Man calls the *fruit of his labor*—and thus pay his tax from a larger income. Second, it would be fair, for it is no more than what we do now—remember Bastiat.

With enormous complication and cost we transpose the individual's value added to myriad points in the economic chain, there to be taxed in unaccountable and often incomprehensible ways. It is only a chimera that the individual does not carry this burden now. If we want to understand our individual tax burden, we need do no more in any nation than to sum all taxes, fees, and costs imposed by the stationary bandit and divide these by the number of us within the nation. Trees, trucks, and towers cannot *pay* any tax. *We* pay the tax. Let this once be understood, and we shall come to the great advantage of the thing: we shall be thrifty, for we shall see every drop of sweat we give up for what we buy. The last thing the stationary bandit wants, and he will fight us tooth and nail for it, is that we should truly come to understand his cost to us. He knows that should this ever pass, the game will be up. No more golden chariots; no more palaces; no more wine, women, or song. It'll be bread and water for him. Let us not imagine that he will easily give up his princely ways.

Now, in 2010, we see the stationary bandits moving from the fiction of equitable taxation—long years gone—to outright theft. We have become so inured to this form of depredation that we are as weary as an old whore, allowing defilement by whatever gangster comes along for whatever bits of copper may be thrown at us. Faced with a financial panic largely of their creation, governments pissed themselves collectively and emptied their treasuries to affect a cure. Whether the cure will prove worse than the disease remains to be seen. In flight training, the recommendation is given, should one become disoriented and confused, to simply let go of the controls; the plane will fly itself. It might have been far better to let go of the controls in the 2008–2009 panic. It's not done yet. Faced with empty treasuries, unconstrained spending, and frighteningly worsening deficits, the stationary bandits are choosing to impose all manner of "emergency" and "temporary" taxes, absolutely without reason or law; they are stealing wherever they can, trying to mug a sufficient number of people in so many different ways that the scale of the theft may pass unnoticed. They have chosen two targets: the people at large, for multiple incremental taxes and fees, and the "fat cats"—well, the perceived fat cats, anyway—because the bandits feel they can get away with it at the polls. After all, it's all the fat cats' fault, isn't it?

But all these taxes have no sense to them, no hint of just application, no whisper of legality. They are theft. The people, still afraid, will tolerate them. Were these monstrous tax increases to have to be levied on individual incomes, they would provoke a rebellion, and perhaps not a very civil one at that—pitchforks and pikes, methinks.

As the second wave of the panic builds, as it comes to be seen that our governments are *insolvent*, the people will understand in a harsh and unequivocal manner the logic of Bastiat's wisdom. The politicians will, of course, demonize the fat cats. If we are very fortunate the people will realize that government itself has betrayed them. The people will not realize that they themselves animated the betrayal, that they ignored one more inviolable economic law that is taught even to children: you cannot have your cake and eat it too. By insisting that government remain bloated—and we do—we have created a situation in which there is not, structurally and permanently, enough money to pay the bills. For a time, the politicians will pretend that if the rich were not so rich, the poor would not be so poor. Philosophically and mathematically, this is a canard, the lie repeated by bloviating demagogues since time began. It can only be true in an oligarchy, where the government and a few families of privilege form a cabal to rape the land—a cabal that could not exist without the power of the state. This has long been the pain of South American countries. The mixing of public and private monies is a deadly brew, a recipe for oppression, and a guarantee of general poverty.

Our public finances are in disarray. The system whereby the politicians use public monies to ensure their positions has reached its end point. Something must now give. Either the people must accept a reduction in their prosperity, or the stationary bandit must go on a diet. Which will be ascendant is not easy to discern. One may hope that the world will be led out of the mire by new nations, or at least newly rising nations like China, who will keep to a truer path for now and set us the good example. We, who want everything but not to pay for it, have a lesson to learn. The win-win option would be to slash government with a draconian hand and to put thereby a large number of unproductively employed persons into productive employment. The combined effect would be startling.

What would "slash" realistically mean? Let us think practically: a five-year freeze on new hires for *all* levels of government. No one is fired. We let attrition do the job. And we don't have to contemplate the impossible, the retraining of government employees for productive work. The public enthusiasm for the thing would build as the benefit accrued. A second five-year commitment would do only more good, by which time public employment would be down more than a third. Lest anyone doubt, let us ask this: if tomorrow we awoke to a world from which half of our public employees had vanished, assuming some *deus ex machina* automaton replaced the idle hordes in motor vehicle bureaus, would we notice it?

Simultaneously, the reduction in functionaries would oblige, with the greatest benefit, a systematic reduction in regulation. We do not speak of those rules by which we ensure a reasonable order in society—always the ones the defenders of regulation point to—but the impossible and often incomprehensible maze of rules that complicate our lives and achieve nothing, save shackling us. The federal tax code exceeds ninety thousand pages. What sane person could not reduce it to ninety pages? How about *one* page, or a few lines? Here's a single sentence suggestion: each person shall annually pay a tax equivalent to 20 percent of his income, subject only to a deduction of $15,000 per dependent, himself included—a deduction which shall be annually adjusted for inflation. Interestingly, every IRS commissioner of the last two decades has asked Congress to simplify the tax code—surprised?—entirely without effect.

We do not have to ask why. It is the chief vote buying apparatus of our scoundrels in Congress!

We are entering this endgame of sorts as players without chips at a roulette table where no color wins. The drinking is done, the hangover fated. There's no booze left, only a bit of bad moonshine with which to prolong the fun. The stationary bandits are beside themselves, their mad plans in desperate tatters, their glow gone, the snake oil spent. They won't go down easily. We are witnessing before our eyes the conversion of our comfortable and somewhat benign democracies into regimes bearing far too many of the hallmarks of despotism and totalitarianism. The first step—we are told—is that we must suffer for our sins, but curiously absent from the prescription for pain are the princes and their minions. They will keep their castles, thank you very much, while the heat goes off in the huts. This is not only metaphorical. Most of us have noticed that while we are asked to "turn down the heat and wear sweaters," our public spaces ever more nearly resemble the tropics. Apparently public thermostats do not go to 68°F (20°C). There is no end to the hypocrisy. We listen to all the pap about energy conservation, "carbon footprints," and adjusting our lifestyles while our princes blithely carry on. We stand for it. We accept, toothless, numb, and dumb. It is hard to represent that slavery is not man's natural state.

We are seeing signs that those attentive to history may discern with concern. Governments are levying taxes at an unprecedented rate when they should be cutting them. We know from hard experience where this leads: a protracted period of financial malaise, of economic distress. No, we won't starve. But we also will not prosper. The only growing sector will be the public one, but only to sustain itself, entirely without benefit to us.

The levies are now overtly political. Recently in the UK (2009) the government has proposed to increase pensioners' payments temporarily—at a time of no cost-of-living rise—and the term for the temporary increase is curiously aligned with the period until the likely next general election. Is it not perfectly transparent what is going on? The reactions should also be of concern. The disdained fat cats in finance are to become subject to a supra-tax of 50 percent on bonuses in excess of £25,000, and they have responded to this proposed plunder exactly correctly, telling the government to take care, for their activity and their domiciles are portable. They can move. They aren't quite serfs. Of course, the stationary bandit may counter with the American approach and formalize their serfdom. An American citizen can (still) move, but he cannot escape the tribute due the stationary bandit. So long as he is a citizen, wherever he may live, wherever he may labor, never mind whether for a decade or a lifetime, he shall owe taxes to the United States. Why? Is he property? Apparently, yes. He is bound for life.

The economic lesson that *public greed* teaches us is that those in power will always pretend that the money they take from us is spent for us, for our own good; with it they will create marvels. No doubt. Versailles, the Kremlin, the Forbidden City, and Topkapi are marvels, but marvels built on the backs of slaves. Even at the level of an American village—my own very silly one—we face a coterie that wants us to have, at huge expense, a town hall "of which we can be proud." The only pride a free man wants for his town hall is in its modesty. Our roads are falling apart, a scene from an Al Gore horror movie; our public sewer system is literally bursting at the seams; and all our princes have in mind is a gilded town palace! If it's a plaque the bastards want, let us get them a headstone.

Public greed, as the insightful British minister understood more than a century ago, would be the downfall of democracy. When Presidents Bush and Obama urged—wisely or unwisely—emergency measures to confront the 2008–2009 financial panic, Congress could not act without adding over eight hundred special spending provisions, every single one of them to buy votes. Think about this. Faced with a grave and dangerous crisis, these scoundrels would not act for us without putting themselves first. It is the utter degeneration of our republic, the morals of the public sector suborned by lucre. It is the drug addict who, confronted with his own demise, cannot resist another jab.

Forget private malfeasance, no matter how objectionable! Compared to the sins of the public sector, the massive and made-legal corruption of our stationary bandit, the private sector's transgressions are but small change. What is the size of the public scandal? It isn't very hard to assess in a rough-and-ready way. Take away all the wants and leave the needs. In all our Western democracies, this will mean starting with the half of our GDPs given over to the public sector and cutting it by half, leaving one quarter. There it is, more or less: one quarter of our economies is devoted to public waste. The astonishing thing is that the donkey's back bears the burden. What might the little beast do without it?

We have come, through our intravenous public sector, to need it as a drug. Within the memory of those who are grandparents today, we did not require it. In the 1960s, the United States began a vast program of social assistance, mimicking the route many European countries had already followed. The proportion of the population said to live "below the poverty line" was given as 20 percent. Half a century and many trillions of dollars (a veritable Mississippi-in-flood of money) later, the proportion living below the poverty line is, ahem, 20 percent. A work of genius! Any economist will tell us that we constructed a system that created and institutionalized as much poverty as ever we alleviated. The money we are speaking of is today called "entitlements," which somehow implies that someone is entitled to it—a perversion of meaning. These programs were conceived to buy votes. In that regard, they have been effective, but in virtually no other. To institutionalize poverty is cruel. No?

Politicized and excessive taxation to support the stationary bandit's bread and circuses *distorts* the function of markets and *penalizes* society—all citizens—in ways unexpected, obscure, and pernicious. Take death duties. They are a relatively easy sell because, once again, they are born primarily by the conveniently disdained fat cats. But do they not attack the very foundation of private right and private property, the twin notions so essential to liberty? Ultimately and inevitably, we are all touched. Let us look now at one of the most nefarious and injurious consequences of the inheritance and gift tax.

In the United States, we have been much concerned of late with what the media have painted as rogue corporations and banks that by their relentless greed have put us all at risk. A simple question therefore: among these bad guys, how many are *privately owned*, not publicly listed? Yeah, very few, if any. Why? Because a privately owned company will be governed by the owner's self-interest, implying a natural prudence and care. The risk of the joint stock company has been long known. Those who take the risk are not those whose money is at risk, and ever more so. Publicly traded companies are managed by hired guns whose sole interest is to line their pockets. Some, for not all are without integrity, do their level best. Others are just out to take from the owners as much money as they are able, as quickly as possible. You will not find the outrageous salaries the press and politicians so like to bawl about in privately owned companies. No private owner would pay them! They occur in publicly traded companies because the owners, the shareholders, are so fractionalized that they exercise no effective control. The board sets the salaries, but the board is a body polluted with incest at the directorial level; I rub your back, you rub my back. A publicly traded company is as a farm the owner leaves in his tenants' hands while he goes off to the big city to live. He is a fool if he thinks they will long preserve the farm's revenue for him. But these are just the symptoms.

What is the root of the illness? It is the inheritance tax. In the United States, we have made the long-term holding of a company by a private family all but impossible. The tax is so great upon the death of the founder that the company must be sold to pay it. And thus our most successful private companies pass into the madhouse of the stock market, of managements disconnected from the long-term responsibility for the companies, the private care that would keep them good and stable employers for the many. There was once a sumptuous jackass in American business—not the only one by any means—who was given the moniker "Chainsaw Al." What Chainsaw Al did was to savage an old and well-established company, the Scott Paper Company, giving the illusion of great success. Anyone can do this who is willing to destroy a company. You gut it, you pump up profits for a few months, you sell it quickly—"flip it," in the jargon—and you leave town, before it collapses. Think of it as a rocket. You can save fuel by shutting down the engine, and the thing will continue on its trajectory for some distance. It seems you have performed magic. But then it falls. The key is to eject before the fall. Chainsaw went from Scott to work his magic at Sunbeam, another venerable and respected firm. After he scuttled the structure, the house fell so fast he didn't make it out in time. He went from hero to horse's ass, a transformation never more justified. But he made off with millions. No private owner would have allowed Chainsaw into the house!

There it is, plain and simple: not only does the death duty tax money that has already been taxed—an immoral act by any standard—but it also distorts the function of the market by causing owners to construct elaborate schemes to protect their interests, to imagine structures that only make sense in the face of a draconian tax, and ultimately to take public any truly successful company. It is true that an owner can become very rich through a public listing. It is also true that owners prefer to remain owners. It is a very old and durable instinct to keep what one has. We like to hand things down. Isn't that a fair right? If it is not, we are saying that there is no property but that which the stationary bandit temporarily grants, giving him thereby a broad license and a dangerous power. It means we entirely cede our rights and our liberty and enjoy these only at the prince's pleasure. Indeed we find our politicians often speaking with reproach of those who "don't pay their fair share," but omitting to say that all has been paid that was legally due. I wonder if our pontificating politicos pay more tax than legally obligated? This is class warfare, one of the lowest and most dangerous forms of politics that can be practiced. It is a demagoguery that leads to despotism.

Let us consider the very notion of property. Can we not agree that what we have fairly earned is ours, and ours completely, such that the only way it may be taken from us is by due process of law, implicit in which is the notion that the taking is a punishment for a generally agreed malefaction? That, absent this malefaction, our property is ours to keep and to dispose of? It was so for much of the life of our republic. The founders would cry to know it is no longer.

Liberty without property does not exist. A slave with property does not exist. He is a free man. Property *manumits*. In our Western democracies, in our votocracies, where the buying of votes is the principal object of our politicians, in order to perpetuate their power, each decade sees the right of property eroded. It is at the point now where the popular notion in many of our Western democracies is that the one who has more than his fellows is somehow a thief, a not quite honest man. Our politicians encourage the view, wanting all the geese plucked to the maximum extent. Bad news for them: plucked geese don't lay eggs, and surely not golden ones. In a society in which property is not sacred, liberty will be transitory. Property is the root of liberty.

The distortion wrought upon us by the inheritance tax, causing good and well-cared-for private companies to enter the stock market, is large and universal. It is yet more proof that no law touches only one. There is no such thing as a tax levied upon one that is not paid by all. In the case of the inheritance tax, the price paid directly, in cash, is small compared to the damage wrought upon the economy. Underlying the whole thing is a fundamental question of morality and liberty. Is what a man has fairly earned his? Does liberty still matter?

Two further considerations must be addressed regarding the inheritance tax and its twin, the gift tax. First, the notion that you cannot freely give what is yours is antithetical to common sense, to any reasonable understanding of ownership and property. If a farmer cannot give a cow to his son, who is trying to set himself up on his own, there is something in it which makes us ask, "Why the hell not?" It's his cow, isn't it? A petty commentator will miss the point entirely and counter that the farmer can gift it to his son, provided the value doesn't exceed a certain amount each year—an amount made derisory by inflation. But once again liberty is not made of a stuff that can be parsed; it is either whole or it is not. If a man cannot freely give what is his, is it really his? And if it isn't his, or completely his, we redefine property, by law, as a temporary thing. The liberty of which property is the guarantor becomes temporary as well.

Second, let us consider the effect of this "tax on a tax"—a construct we generally consider wrong—on the earnings of a man. In the United States (2009), it doesn't take much for a man to effectively pay 40 percent of his income in taxes, "all told." In our fellow Western democracies that figure is well above 50 percent. Setting aside for a moment the justice of taking half a man's labor for the state, let us follow the money when the man dies, or wishes to give it to a son or daughter, whereupon it will be subject to a further 50 percent tax. (I am treating the current bizarre rate structure as an aberration that will soon be changed.) Finally let us add inflation at a modest rate of 2 percent per annum and assume that the money was earned ten years prior to death or gift. Therefore:

Earned	$1.00
Effective tax (40%)	$0.40
Net income after tax	$0.60
10-year interest income (3% pre-tax, 1.8% after tax)	$0.195
Inflation @ 2% p.a	$0.129
Net Value after 10 years	$0.666
Gift or Death Tax @ 50%	$0.333
Net after tax	$0.333

We won't follow the money through successive generations, but it will all but disappear. Let's keep to a single generation: father to son, mother to daughter. Of the dollar fairly earned, two-thirds is taken by the state. Slave or free?

The argument advanced by those of a socialist inclination, but who nonetheless have the decency to be made uncomfortable by this arithmetic, is that the calculation I have presented only applies to relatively wealthy individuals—that it is incorrect for the great majority of us, themselves happily included. This is akin to saying that a mad dictator who limits his arbitrary executions to every tenth man is not too bad from the standpoint of the other nine. Also, it ignores Bastiat: the tax paid falls upon each and every one of us.

Let us now contemplate tax havens, the new bête noire of stationary bandits worldwide. The catastrophe for liberty that IT has wrought is that the stationary bandits can now gang up against us all. There will soon be nowhere left to go to be free. The press, whose understanding of economics would generally make a first-grader's understanding of quantum mechanics seem impressive, have gloried in the stationary bandit's pursuit of tax havens. We shall take two views, for both have merit.

First, drawing from Plato's *Republic*, we learn the concept of civic duty—basically, in this instance, the biblical injunction to "render unto Caesar what is Caesar's." There is such a thing as civic duty, and it underlies any orderly society, the existential goal being the blessing of good government. The devil is in the dose, and it is a great devil. Most of us would judge that an orderly society that brings us commonly agreed elements of common need, and which does so constrained and safeguarded by a constitution, would merit our contribution. A figure of one-fifth of our incomes will seem a not only just but economically beneficial contribution. It comes up repeatedly in economic studies as a threshold figure—notably Milton Friedman's Nobel Prize–winning work. Should I represent that the cost of an orderly society shall be 90 percent of our incomes, I will have a revolution on my hands; most of us will understand it for a bad deal. Thus we have begun to bracket the thing, understanding that 10 percent might not get the job done and 90 percent is too much. I will suggest further that most of us would say that half is also too much; an orderly society should not cost us half of our life's labor, and historically it does not. The historical reference point is a good one, asking just what orderly societies cost in the past. We do not have to go any further back than the quite recent and quite modern nineteenth century to understand that the thing could be done for less than 15 percent of a nation's income. We can find examples of thrifty and efficient governments well into the twentieth century—Switzerland, for example. Friedman studied the subject perhaps more exhaustively than any of his fellows and found that state spending up to about 20 percent of the nation's income brings advantage to the nation, but there beyond disadvantage. The stationary bandits, drunk on gold and power, sell us the snake oil of gargantuan government by provoking our fears: if we do not keep them in power and luxury, we shall suffer all the worst catastrophes imaginable. The reality is the contrary.

So, what of tax havens? What is a tax haven? For a serf in the Middle Ages, it would have been a dark corner in a cellar where he might have put a few turnips by to see his family through the winter. They were his master's due, but he managed to tuck a few in some sacking and get them away. By law, he committed a crime. We do not begrudge it to him. Our sympathies are entirely with the miserable wretch, not at all with his master. Yet he is a thief, and he has hidden the food he stole. Discovered, he might have been put to death.

In the case of a modern tax haven, there are ordinarily the following differences. First, in the popular imagination, only fat cats—greedy and dishonest fat cats, at that—would use a *foreign* tax haven. This fans Americans' long distrust of everything foreign, and our demagogues play it to the hilt. Second, contrary to the serf who *stole* the food he hid, the money found in modern tax havens was most often fairly *earned*. The notion we find in the press, with innuendo about crime and dark dealings, is one that has been created by the stationary bandit demagogically playing to some of our worst instincts: envy, egalitarianism, and tribalism.

Our legislators, ever busy vote shopping, have created a long list of legal tax shelters for their pals. Need we speak of agricultural policy, a dark elephant in our Western democracies? An intricate web of regulations and favors that results in such absurdities as paying farmers *not* to plant their land ... with our money? Or vast programs of tax credits and subsidies for which there is no need—demand and price being self-evident—for the production of foodstuffs, milk for example? What about energy policy, that miasmic swampland of gifts, grants, and goodies, ostensibly to encourage the production of energy? Why would not the free market achieve this through the quest for gain? There is no such thing in economics as a demand for which there is no supply. Congress has created tax havens all around us, complex and often incomprehensible structures whereby those they mean to favor are blessed, all in the pursuit of votes.

Know what's wrong with the much castigated "offshore" tax havens? One, they are offshore. Two, they are useless for the buying of votes. Three, they allow free men to remain free, away from the stationary bandit's grasp. Of course the stationary bandit is in a rage; he lusts for his lucre. The sanctimony is only demagoguery, playing to envy and egalitarianism, to make us cheer the bandit on. *If the burden of taxation were reasonable and just, there would be no tax havens.*

I do not, I hope, only rant against the excesses of government. Good government is a blessing. But most of us are skeptical that good government can anymore exist. We have forgotten the great wisdom of Thomas Jefferson that the government that governs least governs best. We have been stuffed with so much pap that this sage advice seems now somehow unsuited to our times. There is no such thing as a large government that governs well—never was, never will be. Size is waste. Size is corruption. Size is power. Size is arrogance. This is the equation. It does not allow for any other solution. All of history tells us this. Size in government is serfdom in the people.

We cannot overlook that large government is also wasteful government. As regards the inherent waste, the statement requires little explanation; it is so apparent and so widely recognized that further comment would be superfluous. There is, however, a less often considered side of the thing that demands our attention, the waste that exists in the economy only to fend off the lustful grasp of government. Imagine the armies of lawyers, accountants, financial advisors, regulatory compliance staffs, and supporting camp followers required just to keep oneself "on the right side of the line." This is *unproductive* labor on a vast scale, required not by any sound economic need but by way of protection. It is as much *protection money* as that taken by the Mafia. In this case it is a mafia created and empowered by government. Knowing that some three-quarters of our legislators are lawyers is not encouraging to us. They have only ever voted the advantage of their profession. Yet we are not angry.

Lastly we come to the matter of unintended consequences, with a terrible financial and societal cost. We have already spoken of this in various ways. Earlier in this chapter we examined the trillions of dollars spent on social welfare in the United States—and all of the other Western democracies—without the least effect upon the proportion of us who live in poverty. This is a direct cost, one that can be calculated by an accountant. What has been the cost to society, the one we do not and cannot measure, of the tens of millions of children's lives ruined by the condemnation of their parents to a welfare prison—of the crime-, illness-, drug-, and booze-dazed wastelands of public housing, to the bombed-out schools from which nary a student can have a fair chance? Yes, these are the unintended consequences, with a cost that has become far greater than we can count with only money.

We do not need to go much into our past for the nightmare of the Volstead Act, an act that ostensibly was going to transform us—against all human experience—into teetotalers, but which in fact gave organized crime its purpose, its investment, and its foundation. Today, read "War on Drugs" in the place of "Volstead Act." This "war" of extraordinary stupidity—or venality—has doubled violence across the land and subsidized the greatest increase in organized crime since, well, the Volstead Act. It wasn't good enough to do it once, was it?

In the theme of the day, the matter of "alternative energy"—basically uneconomical energy made interesting to cagey investors by government subsidy—we already see the tortuous evolution: childish enthusiasm for ethanol followed by the adult realization that the production of all that grain has consequences: higher corn prices, transformation and expansion of agricultural lands, pressure for deforestation, increased consumption of what across much of America is a limited supply of water, burgeoning chemical fertilization. Oh. Didn't think of all that, did we? Moreover, the damned stuff consumes as much energy to produce as it yields—a proper work of genius. It is only incidental that ethanol is also damaging to engines. Government will never be able to avoid the unintended consequences of its actions, consequences often greater than the problem.

The free market can also err, but it will correct its course quickly and fluidly. It must. There will not long be the money to support a failed investment. When a man establishes an ice delivery service in the Arctic and fails, it does not hurt us. When the government does it, it is our unvarying experience that the service will be continued well beyond its moment of self-evident failure, possibly forever. If the government had made buggy whips, we'd still be making them today. The self-congratulatory Priuses[6] of film stars and environmentalists' bicycles would have whip marks on their flanks to show for it! Perhaps we could get these sanctimonious souls into self-flagellation, so they might bugger off from beating us. What, by the way, has made film stars who cannot correctly write out the number that represents their annual incomes authorities on just about everything? Have we lost our minds?

We have spoken of taxes and abuse. Now we must speak of collapse. It is a historical verity that high taxes and widespread corruption are symptomatic of the ends of empires. Ibn Khaldūn understood it six centuries ago, Alessandro Manzoni four centuries ago, and Adam Smith three centuries ago. The one—high taxes—implies the other—corruption. These dead white males are not insignificant or irrelevant to our modern world. We will ignore economic laws at the same peril as we would ignore physical laws.

The question whether we are, in our Western democracies, on the point of collapse is an open one. I am not given to faintheartedness or fearmongering. I do not think we are on the point of collapse. I do think we are nearer the point, even if in our developed world it may not have quite the same meaning as in the past. I do not expect famine. On the other hand, on our present course, we must expect that our days of leading the world in technology and prosperity are numbered. The Chinese dragon presses our retreat from center stage, and India sings the chorus. Counting between them half the world's people,

---

6   Prius (n.): Film star's photo-op car while the Hummer is kept in the garage, next to the Ferrari. Al Gore doesn't have this option. He doesn't fit in a Prius. In any case, as he has explained to us, special people as he and his family have special needs. How silly it was of us serfs to have thought otherwise!

these two great nations will likely assume their places at the head of the performance within the next three decades. China, for all its make-believe communism, is in many ways an economically freer nation than our Western democracies. As ever freedom will win.

The twenty-first century will come to be seen as an Asian century. Is it necessary for us to falter for that to be? Does prosperity not always engender hubris and sloth? It often has. Must it? Probably yes. The golden age of a nation-state seems to begin as adolescence yields to adulthood. It may seem ironic to speak of one of the world's oldest nations—China—as youthful, but of course we refer to its rebirth after the dark and terrible era of totalitarian communism, during which it all but died.

The game, however, is not yet played out. The United States, throughout her history, has demonstrated a remarkable capacity for renewal. I believe, however, that this ability was born of liberty, and I would not bet that sufficient liberty remains to see the nation to a new page yet again. The Western democracies of Europe no longer have any tolerance for pain, and in shunning all pain, they have atrophied their muscles. One can judge this from Europe's incapacity to reach decisions in difficult circumstances, as in its shameful hand-wringing during the Kosovo tragedy. It was the United States that acted, in a matter that ought properly to have been attended to by Europeans. Europe today is averse to risk and intolerant of consequences; the old girl still has gums, but no teeth. The European perspective is that this represents a further and more benign—thus superior—evolution of society. What they will discover is that the winner has teeth and a willingness to use them.

It is not the purpose of this chapter to discourse upon international affairs, but to inquire into the collapse of empires through high taxation and the consequent corruption. If China and India rise today, it is because both are *freeing* their markets and *empowering* their *individual* citizens to pursue their happiness as they judge best. This is the remarkable engine described by Adam Smith—the very same engine the founders of the American republic so ably harnessed for the nation they forged. Thus the United States became the most successful nation in the history of the modern era. Liberty animated the young country as it bounded forward, astonishing the world exactly as Edmund Burke had predicted. But success is both elixir and poison, recalling the fatal words of Monte Cristo: one drop heals, two drops kill.

Let us keep those three italicized words in mind: *freedom, the individual, empowered.* Let us once forget them, and we shall rue our bad memory. We shall pay the price. For the moment, the abundance created by individuals empowered by freedom masks the full extent of our loss. It will not be ever so.

Life is about choices. Those who fear to make clear choices forgo their ability to lead. Nature favors leaders. Liberty is neither easy nor without cost. A society that pledges that none shall fall is humane but unwise, for it will lose the very capability that allowed it to make the pledge, and more will thus come to suffer. When we make winners of losers by our generosity and artifice, we make losers of winners. It doesn't work. As Lincoln said, you cannot benefit the poor by bringing down the rich. Honest labor is the source of all worldly reward, and when sloth comes also to be rewarded, honest labor is debased. We saw this throughout the ultra-high tax world, where decent citizens of industrious inclination came to the only logical conclusion they could: Why bother? The shiftless do no worse than we.

The soft and the unwise will bemoan what they disdain as the law of the jungle. Let them. The key word is "law," for so it is. Nature has dealt us this card. We must play the game with it; no one ever found a way not to. It doesn't mean that we cannot be humane and charitable. It means that charity will serve us better when it is private, for therefore fewer will require our charity, and we shall preserve thereby our capacity to be charitable. When our states are bankrupt, as almost all of the Western democracies are, what charity we offer is done only with borrowed money—a terrible tax upon future generations. Which Western government today has balanced accounts? It isn't true that one can forever live on borrowings. Money neither falls from heaven nor grows on trees. It must be earned by man's individual labor and thrift. All else is a Ponzi scheme in which the citizens are compelled to join by the force of the state. Their savings will be debased, and they will thus not be allowed out of the tyrant's grasp. The state, to keep the play going, will tax ever more viciously and will impose ever more draconian penalties upon those who seek to protect themselves from the plunder.

In the United States it is less risky to commit murder, with a smaller chance of being apprehended, than to be charged with a tax offense. The stationary bandit no longer cares about his original pact with us—that he ought to provide protection for our persons—and gives over his entire effort to maintaining his revenue. We spoke of our police, who today are far busier throughout our Western democracies issuing traffic citations whose sole purpose—now openly avowed—is revenue, while ignoring burglaries and all manner of crime, responding to violence against us with nonchalance and ennui. Governments today are in one business only: perpetuating themselves. The rest is snake oil. This is the stage of which Ibn Khaldūn warned: the end-of-empire rape of the people by draconian taxation. It takes higher and higher rates of taxation to maintain the stationary bandit in his splendor; the nation's strength is sapped and her will is broken.

There is more money to be made in deals and corruption than through honest labor. Windmills sprout across the land and make quick-witted opportunists rich. What do they care that the landscape comes to be littered with rusting junk? It is easy money, and one can even receive plaudits from the chattering classes while fleecing the people. It wasn't any different at the ends of the Roman and Ottoman empires. These two very great empires at their apogees led the world, not only in prosperity and expanse, but also—it is too often overlooked—in the liberality of their rule. The tyranny came later. Thereafter they declined and ultimately fell, the weight of the bloat too much to bear. How much bloat can we take? How much better off might we be half so fat? Collapse? Not yet. But check the wall. See the writing.

Chapter 11

Palestine: A Human Tragedy, a Foreign- Policy Wreck

Through the misinformation and naiveté of the people, and the unwisdom, incapacity, and corruption of their leadership, 9/11 traumatized America.

The American people have been uniquely misinformed among the world's peoples regarding the Palestinian situation, through the enormously successful propaganda campaign waged by the Israeli state and its American operatives. This effort has been so well orchestrated that even the inevitable questions were artfully anticipated and recast to Israel's favor. Faced with the world's universal condemnation of Israeli behavior, Americans were primed to imagine the entire world anti-Semitic.

Through this slanted view, America became the active agent of Israeli policy, a participant in a war that has nothing to do with Israel's preservation and everything to do with Israel's expansion—all to America's, the world's, *and* Israel's enormous detriment. The naiveté to which I refer is not the isolationist penchant America has always had, but the newfound one, post Vietnam, whereby Americans wanted no pain, and by which any small pain came to be magnified to unbearable proportions. There were two ways to see 9/11: one as America did, the other as a criminal act that killed fewer people than the average flu does in a month. We not only overreacted, but we reacted wrongly, with huge and enduring moral cost and financial burden to the nation.

Successive American administrations, Democrat and Republican, have been corrupted by the unhappy instrument of Israeli propaganda and influence. I do not propose to be subtle. The Israelis have gotten a wire around the delicate parts of virtually every single member of our Congress. Tel Aviv has only to give a small tug to elicit a prompt and obedient "amen" chorus. Thus they have sold their expansionism as security and their war of oppression against the Palestinians as a war on terror, the perfect complement to America's—notably G. W. Bush's—wars. Hitler, too, waged a war on terror in Czechoslovakia and Poland, only he didn't get the world to see it his way. We know today that to America's great dishonor, much of the information that has underpinned our actions since 9/11 has been as manufactured and as false as that which Germany concocted in 1938–1939 as the rationale for the invasion of its neighbors.

America's misinformation has a stamp: Made in Israel. We may hope, with the Obama presidency, to have finally found a leader who understands the reality of the situation. It remains to be seen. There is at least reason to think that, compared to his predecessors, he better understands the nature of the conflict and the risk it has created globally to American security.

On the other hand, as of this writing there seems to be a willingness to consider military action against Iran, which would be no better than Iraq II. The Israelis have wanted this for years. By the corruption of our leadership for over a generation, we have been made belligerents in Israel's war of expansion and oppression. September 11, 2001 was not an attack. It was a counterattack. To this day, very few Americans understand this. The world understands it however.

By the pursuit of a policy that is not ours, not just, and not intelligent, we have created, perpetuated, and exacerbated a dangerous situation across the world. Our true interest in the Middle East ought to be nothing more than free trade and friendship with all. Instead, we have committed our lives and our fortunes to Israel's expansionist cause. We need to understand that in the pursuit of Israel's policy, we have lost our soldiers' lives and gained the enmity of the world; we have emptied our treasury; and we have prepared the ground for continuing global crises. The 2008–2009 financial meltdown is only the most recent of these. The Bush administration was so worried that the economy would collapse after 9/11—a startling lack of cool under fire—that it opened the floodgates at the Federal Reserve, making the nation awash with easy money. The result was predictable.

Reacting to 9/11 with a global war on terror created the war. Without this unwise declaration, we faced grievous but isolated criminal incidents, which ought to have been treated as the Oklahoma City bombing was treated, or as the United Kingdom treated the bombings during the Irish troubles. Of course we had to act. We had, for example, to restore the intelligence capacity the nation lost during the Clinton administration. And we had to be willing to hunt down and to kill, with the same determination the Pinkerton men brought to the pursuit of Butch Cassidy, the terrorists—here finally a correct use of the word— who might launch further attacks. This was not the Afghan nation, and it most certainly was not the Iraqi nation, and it isn't the Iranian nation. In Iraq, we attacked, by the suggestion and manipulation of Israel and its supporters at the heart of the Bush administration, a nation uninvolved in acts against the United States and with no capacity to threaten us.

In Afghanistan, we properly acted against a regime that had aided and abetted those who engineered 9/11, but we then stepped into a protracted war that *cannot* be won in any meaningful sense. We will not bring our version of order and peace to Afghanistan, and we will not stop Afghanistan from being one of the world's major drug producers. No one has ever succeeded, and we will not. We have violated every wise counsel given by Sun Tzu two millennia ago. "Do not engage in long foreign wars, for no matter the circumstances of the people whose land you invade, they will in time turn against you, and your adventure will lose the support of your own people." Ah. We might have learned that

165

from Vietnam. Sun Tzu further admonished that foreign wars must have a clear and achievable purpose. Ah.

Now, as of this writing, President Obama has ordered a substantial increase to the number of troops in the theater. Afghanistan has 24 million people, Pakistan 132 million. Some 5 million Afghan refugees—the dispossessed are always dangerous—live in camps along the Pakistani border. The land is bleak, mountainous, and hard. We will have 100,000 troops on the ground. What do we think we're going to accomplish?

We have two legitimate practical purposes and one moral purpose to attend to: first, that further acts against us not be prepared; second, that Pakistan's nuclear arsenal remains safe; and third, that we give some assistance to the people to whom we have brought so much desolation and distress. That's it. Forget nation building—there's no nation as we conceive of one to build. Forget eliminating the heroin production, and really forget bringing democracy to the region. These are nonstarters. In all matters, one must know what one can do and what one cannot. If we would cease being Israel's co-belligerent in the Israeli-Palestinian conflict, we might discover that much of the animus toward us in the Muslim world will evanesce. That would be simpler and more strategic.

This does not mean abandoning Israel or cowering before the enemy. These are only the propaganda tools of the Israeli state. If Israel's case were just, if this war were about the assurance of Israel's existence instead of Israel's expansion, we and the Western democracies could have good reason to stand by Israel. But it's not just, it isn't about Israel's existence, and those we have branded the enemy would not be if we did not oppress and attack them, keeping them in a nightmarish prison of misery, terror, and want. Does it surprise us they do not like us? As I said, Americans have been misinformed and naive.

Lastly we come to what I have called our incapacity in the face of 9/11. The purpose of leadership is to lead. In the place of a commander in chief we got, in the most recent Bush administration, the trembler in chief. The only fair way to say what happened to Bush and his cohorts on 9/11 is Elizabethan: they shit their pants. Leaders don't.

The full history is not yet written. In time, I believe we will come to understand that one group, George Bush among them, was terrified and bewildered, while another group, in whom the president had placed his trust, were wily and cynical, using Bush's disorientation and incapacity to wittingly and deliberately advance Israel's purpose. This group was led by Dick Cheney and included all the neocons, whose strategy was crafted in Israel and advanced by de facto Israeli agents like Wolfowitz, Pearl, Kristol, and Lieberman. History will show it. It is only in the United States, for the reasons already spoken of, that this view is considered anti-Semitic. That blandishment is the red herring of the Israeli government and its lobby in the United States. Fortunately the American Jewish community has begun to understand that they have been used by a militant faction in Israel, playing upon their profound loyalty to the existential notion of Israel, for a purpose with which they are increasingly uncomfortable.

For many the events in Gaza were a watershed. There have always been American Jews, not to mention Israelis, who were horrified by what Israel was doing. The filmmaker and actor Woody Allen has been notable among them for his courage. And slowly, slowly, Americans more broadly have begun to understand. A notable and brave book by the imminently respected political scientists Mearsheimer and Walt[7] broke the silence and detailed the extent to which Israel has infiltrated the leadership of the United States and American public opinion—how the Israeli lobby attacked any dissenting view and ruined the reputations of those who dared to speak. Since publication of that groundbreaking work, articles have appeared in the American press that would never have been published there before; it was no longer automatic anti-Semitism to criticize Israeli policy. This however is all an aside to our asseveration: the American response to 9/11 demonstrated a complete incapacity at the highest levels of our government. The combination of

---

7   John J. Mearsheimer and Stephen Walt, *The Israel Lobby and U.S. Foreign Policy*, (Farrar Straus Giroux, 2007).

misinformation and naiveté in the people with corruption, unwisdom, and incapacity in their leaders has stirred a deadly brew whose cauldron holds portions yet unserved.

Anyone writing that which I have here written exposes himself to virulent personal attacks and false accusations. I am untroubled. I would express the identical opinions about oppression and inhumanity anywhere. There are fundamental errors in our understanding of this Israeli-Palestinian conflict we would do well to address. President Obama, having seemingly grasped the underlying issues and well understood the risk and cost this unresolved conflict poses for the United States, appears desirous to act. Let us hope he will have the strength to see it through.

Some points:

- The conflict is not substantively about religion. Both sides have their religious fanatics, the one as obdurate and moonstruck as the other, but the majority on each side is rather secular.

- The Arabs do not hate the Jews. They may well, with good cause, hate Israelis. The Israeli propaganda has tried to suggest that the Palestinian Arab militancy toward them is, once again, an inchoate holocaust. It isn't. It is an old- fashioned territorial fight.

- Understand that the Palestinians' land was forcibly taken from them by action of the European powers, notably France and the United Kingdom, for the purpose of establishing a "Jewish homeland." How would Americans feel if Mexico seized—we're imagining for a moment that it could—a part of California to establish a "Mexican homeland" for the large number of immigrant Mexicans living there? These sorts of land seizures never go down well. The atavistic attachment of a people to a patch of soil is not historically something to trifle with.

- No one seriously contests the existence of the State of Israel *within* its 1967 borders, the very borders all of the international community and the United States recognize. But residing within those borders is not Israel's purpose. It has been the long-term policy of the Israeli state to keep the region destabilized in the hope that someday, the opportunity will present itself to seize *all* of the land, right to Jordan. This is why Israel will do anything— truly anything—to derail any prospect of peace. The pattern is clear. Iraq was just one move on the chessboard. Iran would be another. Whether this grim game Israel plays will bring it anything is very questionable. As Thomas Friedman has written, Israel is in a quandary because it wants three things but can in fact only have two of the three: first, all of the land of biblical Israel; second, a Jewish religious state; third, a democracy. It is an equation without solution. If it has all of the land, it will have a population that will be in its majority Palestinian, which means that it won't be a Jewish state. Or, if it takes all the land and enforces its religion, it won't be a democracy. It doesn't work. Wise Israelis understand this. Even an Israel within the 1967 borders will ultimately prove problematic, as the Arabs have larger families than the Jews, such that in time they will become the majority. They will *vote* the transformation of Israel ... unless Israel establishes apartheid and does not allow Arab Israelis to vote as full citizens. It's a box without exit. Israel's long-term interest, given the capability of its people, would be to establish itself as a secular state within the 1967 borders, at peace and enjoying prosperity with its neighbors. The integration of Arab Israelis as full and equal citizens is mandatory. There was no historical animosity between Arab and Jew, and there must be none again. It is the land issue that must be settled. And both sides need to deal with their moonstruck contingents. The Palestinians must have their own state, enjoying all of the prerogatives of any sovereign state. All the world's nations have called for this! The problem in the broader region isn't Iran; it's a nuclear armed Israel with an avowedly expansionist policy. (President Obama is the first American president to publicly speak of Israel's large, *and illegal,* nuclear arsenal—by most estimates some 250 warheads. The Israelis were powerfully miffed. Curious, is it not, that Israel's very real illegal arsenal is not considered an appropriate subject for discussion, but Iran's potential and puny future arsenal is? Odd sense of justice in all this, no?)

- The Hamas position that the State of Israel is illegitimate—which the Israelis are very happy for, as it gives them a reason to bully the Americans into not speaking with Hamas, the *democratically elected* government of the Palestinians—is a bargaining chip. Indeed, Hamas has already let on that it is a conditional position. Israeli propagandists and their chorus in the American media make this a call "for the elimination of Israel." It is not. Next.

- The calling of Palestinian militants "terrorists" is a red herring. They may indeed use violence in their fight against Israeli oppression—who would not?—but they are not terrorists. They never attack beyond the immediate conflict area. The Israeli army routinely attacks and terrorizes unarmed Palestinian civilians. Let them call each other what they want, but let us in the international community recognize both sides as militants in a territorial conflict. If we do not, we will continue to take sides, and in taking sides we will ourselves continue to be an obstacle to peace.

- It actually doesn't matter to us what the Israelis want beyond their right to a secure existence within the 1967 borders. What matters to us—enormously—is the elimination of this suppurating infection in the Middle East and the healing of the wounds at the heart of our troubles in the region. *Our* interest is peace. It is time we used our enormous support for the state of Israel—three billion dollars per year and untold hidden bennies—to get our interest advanced. If the Israelis don't like it, well, you're on your own, chaps.

- In using our influence—which means insistence—to ensure that Israel comes to a peaceful resolution of the situation with the Palestinians, we will in fact be doing the Israeli people a great favor. Their massively complex politics don't allow them to get it done. It's time it was done for them. The American Jewish community is increasingly of this opinion. It's now or never for Israel. The birth of every Palestinian child diminishes the urgency of any solution for the Palestinians. They can wait this one out and get everything. But we don't have that long to wait, because we need to get ourselves out of the mire of the Middle East.

- A faction of the Christian right in the United States holds to the view that one of God's promises to man involves the return to Israel of all of its biblical lands. Someone needs to have a talk with these people. They are not only an impediment to peace—Israel uses them gleefully—but complicit in the oppression and suffering of the Palestinians. On both counts, they are risking their eternal souls! We cannot on the one hand bewail religious fundamentalism and on the other bring our homegrown version into our foreign policy. Let all men of goodwill join in the creation of peace in this land, which is holy to Christian, Muslim, and Jew.

The world needs fewer conflicts and we in the Western democracies need to bring an end to this war between cultures that has so exercised us these last ten years. The Muslim world has two legitimate beefs with us: our blind approval for Israel's oppression of the Palestinians and our support of massively corrupt and oppressive Arab regimes. We have a legitimate beef of our own: the cultivation by some Arab countries of a fundamentalist-expansionist version of Islam that seeks to fulfill a dream of world conversion by whatever means. It is naive and not very clever to boot, to think that these issues are unrelated. The Israeli-Palestinian conflict is the infection the extremists use to support their cause. It is the moral wrong that makes even Muslims of peace and goodwill take some satisfaction from extremist acts. It doesn't mean they intellectually agree with them; it does mean there is an understandable emotional support for them. In Northern Ireland, many Catholics who would not have raised a hand against another man nonetheless gave their moral support to the IRA. The Bush administration's view of all those who weren't with us as against us simply made so. The real world isn't so black-and-white.

Our policy must be seen to be bringing, and then to bring, peace to the Israelis and the Palestinians. In the world, Americans alone fail to see the palpable bad faith of Israel and the torture and terror Israel has systematically inflicted upon the Palestinians. This oppression has now been sufficiently detailed, and the parallels to the Nazi oppression of the Jews noted, that it doesn't require additional comment here. Israeli propaganda has been exceptionally well organized in the United States, such that the American people have long seen the conflict the way Israel wanted Americans to see it. The stark reality is otherwise.

So long as the United States continues to pursue Israel's policy, right or wrong, peace will be unattainable. Israel knows that it can always get away with kicking sand in the Palestinians' faces; its American big brother will invariably stick up for it. That's what has to stop. America's interests are not Israel's interests, and America must put its interests and sense of common decency first. George Washington's words come back to us: "Neither too great a friend nor too great an enemy to any foreign power be, for both enslave."

Chapter 12
The Energy Hole

We have already spoken of energy in various contexts; we won't retrace our steps. However, when we speak of energy we must contemplate the imminent lack of it in the Western democracies, France and Japan excepted. The problem isn't any lack of raw material—there's plenty of that—but a rather concerning, not to say frightening, lack of generating capacity. This and the actual state of emissions related to power generation are something for which we have the green children to thank. This is why it's so important that adults take over once more.

It amuses me to hear those of the green cult—I distinguish true conservationists from these—or our ever courageous politicians who follow them, lips at the ready for a kiss at something below waist level, speak of an "emission-free" state when referring to things that are electrically powered, as cars. Where do they suppose the electricity comes from? It might be emission-free had they not stopped modern technology—nuclear technology—for the last thirty years, but they did.

Electricity in most of the Western social democracies is produced by the burning of coal, gas, or petroleum. To charge an electric "emission-free" car requires that a fossil fuel be burned—with emissions—at a generating plant. This "emission-free" stuff is the Alice in Wonderland component of these folk, the unending need to tell themselves fairy tales. If I betray a certain irritation, please understand it as derived from long-standing frustration.

Had our Western world been in the hands of grown-ups these last three or four decades, we would self-evidently have done what the French and the Japanese did: chosen a marvelous new technology—nuclear—which offered quantum advantages versus the old. It was as large a step forward as coal from wood or petroleum from coal. Those who would dissent will inevitably point to Chernobyl and Three Mile Island. Three Mile Island was an incident, not an accident. Chernobyl was serious.

What really happened at Chernobyl? A nuclear plant of a design already at the time considered problematical, maintained with the haphazard attention with which almost all of the Soviet industrial plant was maintained, and attended to by a totalitarian-monopolistic state that never gave human life much value, in effect blew up. The radiation cloud rising from the explosion spread over a large area. People in the immediate danger zone were only evacuated late because it was against Soviet policy to recognize any accident on the premise that a perfect state does not have accidents. But this was one they couldn't keep secret—Geiger counters, you see. At Three Mile Island, the safety procedures and backup systems functioned. There was no threat to public safety. Now, let's look at consequences—the worst case, the very scary "what if"?

Nothing is free. To live is to make trade-offs. One of the infantile perspectives we have come to in our Western world is that this isn't true, that somehow things can be free. Perhaps we're just spoiled brats. Too many things have been free. In the real world, the world governed by nature and nature's laws; actions have consequences. Our objective is to choose the best actions in order to maximize the good and minimize the bad consequences. *There will be risk.* Get over it.

When we draw our electric power from coal-fired plants, we accept the many hazards of mining, the vast energy requirement to extract the coal and to transport it, and the emissions. People die. They just don't die in a single dramatic event. But over time, kilowatt for kilowatt, is the sum so very different? France has operated its nuclear plant, producing four-fifths of her entire electricity, for more than thirty years now without accident. How many would have died if she had produced the same power from coal?

The difficulty with being grown-up in a kindergarten world is that those who tell the truth are excoriated. The children don't want to believe in bad things. They want to sleep snug and tight, aboard the SweetDreams Express. But that isn't reality. Grown-ups don't like bad things any more than the children do … but they know they happen. That is the essence of maturity. Grown-ups also know that everything has a cost, that nothing is free. One must look at things in their sum, on balance, seeking solutions whereby the benefit justifies the cost. It is very much the same debate that occurs across the land when some large expenditure is discussed, a burden upon each individual in the community. Some weepy mom steps forward with the great modern end-all argument: how can you put a price on a life? Well, sorry, lady, but a life has a price. Within our families and between friends, it seems immeasurable—to us, it is—but outside of that circle, it isn't.

This is the problem inherent in our health-care debate, the fact that modern technology allows an almost limitless preservation of life—if not of quality of life—provided one brings a limitless budget to the care. We can't do that. Note to the children: *we do not have a bottomless purse.*

Let us frame this another way, so it isn't tied to evil lucre: which of us would give up half his entire life's labor to save a person we don't know who lives on the opposite coast from us? Tell the truth. The voting booth is private. No one will know. Right. We all know the answer. There is nothing wrong with the answer—not morally, not sensibly, and certainly not as public policy. It is in fact the *only* possible answer.

The price of the modern world is that some of its accidents will shock us more. They will be larger. The new super-jumbo jets carry more than 500 passengers. One will go down in time. The other side of the coin is that millions of passengers travel safely using planes, the *safest* mode of travel yet devised. If the modern world's electricity were all nuclear, we would have to assume that one day, somewhere, there would be the awful accident we do all dread. But we will have powered the world's needs for decades cleanly and securely. The benefit, on balance? Not even close. Nuclear wins, hands down.

One day fission-based nuclear power will be supplanted by fusion-based nuclear power. That day isn't so far off. Those who are inclined to optimism would think the nut will be cracked, at least technically, within a generation; the pessimistic think two or three generations. Only Luddites think it will not be cracked. We cannot have Luddites running our world. We, the great majority of us, do not want to inhabit a Luddite world. The difference between one generation and two or three is minimal to us. Once mankind masters fusion, we shall enter upon a world that will horrify the green kids who have confused environmental goals with their hostility to growth, business, and trade: abundant, clean, and cheap energy, in perfect alignment with the centuries-old curve of the world's energy supply and price, ever more abundant, ever cleaner, ever cheaper.

What we must do for now, for the one or two or three generations required to get us to hydrogen (fusion) power, is to find the interim measures. The energy needs of our modern world, which is an energy- and information-based world, will be met by a combination of improved, new-generation, *and* conservation technologies. (I stress the notion of conservation technologies versus conservation and shall return to that forthwith.) The most abundant and cost-effective current technologies are coal-burning, gas-burning, and nuclear. To the extent that we can choose nuclear, we will assure a cleaner and more stable power base, relatively free from the sometimes uncertain tides of international politics. We can see the mischief that is never far from hand when few control the precious energy needed by many. Ask the Ukraine.

Conservation *technologies* differ from conservation in that they can bring meaningful reductions in our individual energy needs. All energy needs are individual. When they appear not to be—the evil manufacturing plant on the other side of town—they nonetheless are: that plant only exists because we *want* its products. We must stop ducking responsibility; the green children, who use toilet paper as we all do, shouldn't rant against forestry and paper mills, for example.

Whether conservation technologies are more energy-efficient appliances, lightbulbs, houses, cars, or transmission lines—lines from which something over a fifth of our energy is lost!—they are all to our benefit and all well worthwhile. The old rule is good: waste not, want not. As the *free-market* price of energy rises, the incentive to develop conservation technologies rises, and there is no limit to the inventiveness of man.

It is *not* a good idea to try to force the free-market mechanism with artificial constraints, such as taxes that push the price of energy higher. One might reasonably ask why not. It is because the durable energy solution lies in an economic mix of new energy production and conservation. It is not for lack of good intention that no government can improve upon the mix; it is for lack of capacity. Let us reiterate this point: government does not have the ability—the capacity—to correctly improve the mix, and the reason is that whatever government might do, and however intelligent the doers, it will be unable to act on any basis but the current one, and in the real world, this is never static.

Our technology and market conditions change minute by minute, day by day, week by week, and all attempts to anticipate the change will fail, for they cannot factor in the force of *discovery*. As someone has pointed out, no Edwardian supercomputer could have predicted the world of today. The base data would not have been available to the programmer: the advances in physics, chemistry, biology, and medicine. This is why MITI, the Japanese government's technology ministry, though often credited with the Japanese miracle, in fact did the very opposite: it wasted the nation's resources on projects that well-intentioned, smart people *imagined* would be the base for the future, when in fact the future just passed them by.

Planned invention will never create anything but yesterday's invention. True invention is a vital, living thing. Dissenters from this view will point to remarkable and urgent inventions prompted by national need and government, such as the Enigma Project, which cracked the German codes in WWII. The need was clear, but the solution was pure free market. Whoever the wise man was who installed the code breakers, he understood one thing: the experts would never get it. In their place was brought in a ragged group of "minds" from arcane and difficult academic disciplines—the classics, philosophy, languages, mathematics—who were given free rein to explore entirely new ways of understanding codes. And they did.

The solution to our energy needs will most efficiently be found by the market in search of profit. Only those uninstructed in economics will imagine that the market favors a high price for anything. The market favors the lower, *more competitive* (i.e., more efficient) price. See Walmart. What we want and need is the most efficient solution to the energy equation; thus the optimum mix of production and conservation. This mix is never static. It changes daily. It must be allowed to do so, or it will be inefficient by the very next day. Government deals in static concepts, the market in fluid ones. The philosophical difference is profound. To ignore it invites the punishment that ignorance merits.

No market would install a wind turbine or plant corn for ethanol or litter the desert Southwest of the United States with vast arrays of solar panels. Why not? Because they are hugely more expensive than coal, gas, or nuclear energy. As Bjørn Lomborg has pointed out, the solution to our energy needs is not to make energy more expensive—it is to make clean energy less expensive! If Plug A in our house delivers electricity for $0.07 per kilowatt and Plug B for $0.12 per kilowatt, which will we use? Exactly. In the children's magazines, one can read endless silly articles about clean and efficient "green" energy. They are neither. All are so unreliable (wind doesn't always blow, sun doesn't always shine) that they require 100 percent standby generating capacity in traditional plants. As these green energies require that our energy infrastructure be more than doubled, per kilowatt they are often twice or more the cost of traditional supplies *and* oblige the standby capacity—they are anything but efficient and surely not well aligned with the "waste not, want not" axiom. Those who have better mastered good intentions than rigorous thought will immediately seize upon the higher cost as being just what we need to force conservation. They should begin by setting us the good example: no cars, no TVs, no heat, no fridge. And good luck to them. The modern world is energy driven. Most of us want to live in the modern world.

Now the hole. As we touched upon at the beginning of this chapter, we are, in some of our Western social democracies, living on our energy infrastructure of decades ago. New coal-burning, gas-burning, and nuclear plants have been few and far between. In the UK (2009), while the government spins ever more fantastic tales of alternative energy, the plants doing the actual work of powering the nation are aging and rusting. We are rapidly approaching the point at which no time will remain to build new capacity. This will have, if not soon addressed, a critical effect on the economic well-being of those countries that have chosen delusion over investment. It is a very real, very concerning situation. It can still be remedied—the market can act with remarkable speed—but the market must be allowed to act. The politicians need to let the grown-ups take over.

Some will point to China, which faces its own energy challenges, as the proof that the argument I advance is false—that in fact energy shortages are universal. Wrong. The causes are entirely different. China's economic growth, the miracle of the last thirty years, has been so rapid that it has outpaced even China's remarkable rate of energy-plant construction. Miracle? Yes, a human miracle: it has taken hundreds of millions of fellow human beings from hunger and want to relative prosperity. Do we begrudge it? Our shortages—for example in the ever-silly California—are from a childish refusal to confront reality: Californians imagine that they can build no new power plants and have power.

The matter raised, the energy hole, is serious and urgent. It can yet be addressed. It requires a change in public perception and public policy to constrain the endless protests that forestall every new power plant (and, not incidentally, add enormously to their cost ... *our* cost of power). When new technologies are of age, they will offer *advantage* compared to the old, and investment will naturally flow to them. Do we need a better example than the astounding progress in IT, usually brought about by two kids in a garage, to understand the power of invention? Processing capacity has grown exponentially as cost has fallen geometrically. That is the market. Had government taken charge of the thing, we'd be on the seventeenth generation of UNIVACs, a "super" computer the size and cost of a small ocean liner with the computing power of a cell phone.

It is the habit of government—equal parts incomprehension and bad faith—to blame the free market whenever anything goes wrong, accusing in order not to be accused. The reality is different: government actions are often at the root of calamities, not because government is evil but because government is ignorant and inept. The 2008–2009 financial meltdown is an example in point. The politicians were beside themselves to castigate venal bankers and "the failure of the market." In fact, the market functioned rather as could have been predicted. To understand the truth of the matter, we must *follow the money*. There is no such thing as easy credit (i.e., irresponsible lending) without easy money (money untied to responsibility). As we have already discussed, the Bush administration in 2001 opened the floodgates of the Federal Reserve in order to prevent what they imagined might become a grave financial crisis post 9/11. The ensuing flood, never checked, provided the easy money. Easy credit followed as night the day. Were the bankers stupid? Yes. Were they greedy? Yeah, surely. Are human beings inclined to a fast buck when they can get it, *and when the risk to themselves seems small*? Yes, it's economically rational. If we *give* the average honest man a hundred bucks at the tables in Vegas and tell him he has a four in five chance of doubling his money if he will but play, will he play? Yeah. Would you and I play? Yeah. Everything clear? The government meant well but created a global debacle. It remains to be seen whether the presumed solution to the debacle—the bailouts—will not itself engender a further financial crisis. How comes this to affect our dialogue about energy?

Let's begin first with supply. There is no want of basic energy material (fuel) within the foreseeable future—many hundreds of years in fact.

These are the traditional fuels. Moreover, someone needs to explain to unschooled journalists the difference between proven reserves—those that have been found and defined—and ultimate reserves, which are orders of magnitude larger. Why? It does not make economic sense to prove reserves beyond that period for which the investment to do so can provide a reasonable return. That's how the unwitting got caught out in 1974 when they gravely declared that the world would run out of petroleum in seven, ten, fourteen, and twenty-one years (take your pick).

Second, there is some issue with the distribution of fuels across the planet, and we know from history that this can result in serious consequences. The Japanese decision for war in 1939 was at least in significant part a quest for energy. (It was an irony that their war ultimately failed, as Admiral Yamamoto had predicted, for want of fuel.) There is, however, one reassuring factor: the need of a seller to find a buyer. Hugo Chavez can thunder and storm all he wants, but he won't stay long in power if he doesn't sell petroleum. We hear some voices among us—the redneck variety normally—who tell us "the Arabs hate us" and who fear for it. Well, maybe they do and maybe they don't, but whatever it is, they don't hate us enough to commit national suicide for it. Ditto the Russians. What we can get from these unequal distributions of fuels is political pressure and occasional upsets. What we will not get are any durable interruptions of supply.

Third, it isn't true that we in the United States must rely on foreign oil. It is true that we don't want to exploit our energy, preferring to dig in someone else's backyard rather than our own. How long this will make sense is a reasonable question. North America has vast energy reserves.

Fourth, energy is a fungible commodity, meaning that a unit replaces another unit anonymously. Thus, when our war party seeks to convince us that a country will "stop selling to us," they spout economic nonsense. If that country sells energy into the world market—anywhere—it sells to us whether it wants to or not. There is a world market for energy and a world supply, and there isn't a whole lot anyone can do about it, absent temporary dislocations like the Russian one toward the Ukraine.

Fifth, only a hermit in a remote cave could imagine that there will be no major advances in energy technology over the next thirty years, and surely the most extraordinary wonders within the next hundred years. The prophets of doom are inevitably static in their perspective. They take what is and draw a linear extrapolation. That is *never* reality. Never has been. Never will be. The world changes—the natural world and our adaptation to it. Based upon the agricultural capacity of just a century ago, three quarters of our planet's population could not today survive. We innovate. We adapt. We change. Those who traffic in linear extrapolations—remember how AIDS was going to wipe out humanity?—must be ignored. They are silly.

So, what are we worried about? Two things: the upsets that can derive from the distribution of energy and the implications energy production can have for our environment. Both are reasonable questions. For the first, there is a proper role for governments, to recognize that energy distribution concerns and upsets can lead to war and to act in a way to ensure the openness of the global market. As for the second, we cannot today—excepting concerning true pollutants[8] that modern emission technology largely controls—say that we have a problem. There is no clear evidence of a problem, in spite of the concern some have voiced. The concern is reasonable; the reaction has been anything but, based as it is not on the evidence, but on very suspect computer modeling. This modeling is suspect in the first part by the enormous complexity—in a sense, infinite complexity relative to current knowledge—of that which it seeks to model, and in the second part, as we have seen, by the mischief it allows to those who wish to advance one view over another.

Science is largely observational. It makes every sense in the world to observe, but not to react until we know that there is something to

---

8   CO_2 is not a pollutant any more than oxygen is. It is a gas, and as do all naturally occurring gases, it has its part in our planet's makeup—a highly variable part according to our geologic history. Whether it needs to be, or can be, controlled is as yet unknown.

which to react. If there were no harm in the reaction, we might use a precautionary approach, but in fact, there is a vast and global harm to getting this wrong and very little harm to spending some time to better understand things.

As I write, the 2009 Copenhagen Climate Summit has just concluded—an utter failure by rather everyone's view. The commentators, who will soon enough be eating crow (my prediction), are into damage control, blaming the failure on everything but its true cause: the world has ceased to believe in man-made climate change. Thus the stresses between rich and poor are blamed—the rich of course being the guilty party, according to the litany. The stubbornness of China, which is a poor-rich or rich-poor country depending upon one's view, is blamed; the lack of leadership of the United States is also blamed—an easy point for so many reasons that they hardly want reciting; and the "greed over good" mantra of the kiddies survives to fight another day. The headman of Tuvalu—the poster-child island that wants us to believe it will sink, or be submerged—has left crying crocodile tears for his lost land, in fact his lost billions. (The right answer was to tell him that if his island is truly disappearing, he won't need the money, so good-bye.) Anyway, the good news is Tuvalu, a coral island, won't be submerged, as coral adapts to sea level. Their bad news is, they don't need the billions.

The political leaders who gathered in what was to be the Cathedral of Climate Change came up against the cold reality—literally as Copenhagen greeted them with unusually cold temperatures and more December snow than in a generation—and discovered that their crucifix was gone. Thus the discussion turned nasty and political, the usual turn of events when governments talk money.

The hopeful poor passed the collection plate, but the alms given them were more symbolic than real, attached to sufficient conditions that they might be quietly withdrawn later. The kiddies, who did their usual brat act, were beside themselves. They'll soon need a new teddy bear. I am not optimistic that anything will ever extinguish their zeal for a lost spirituality, and they'll just go on to the next cause, pestilential Energizer Bunnies. The global-warming cause will fluidly transform itself into some new mantra, always predicting doom if we do not mend our ways and always promoting some stern pastor to help us to salvation. The theme is ever the same: original sin, guilt and power. Only the circumstances change.

Chapter 13
What if We Could Fix It?

I do not think we can fix it. But let's say we could. Things do change, and over time (the optimist surfaces) they change for the better. What would we do? I suppose many have played at this game—king for a day—but it isn't necessarily trivial to do so. Mankind goes forward by fits and starts.

As we have said in Chapter 1, we in the Western social democracies can see the glass half full. Compared to those of our ancestors, even those in the quite recent past, our lives are good. We are not abject slaves; we enjoy material comfort and even plenty; we have some sense of liberty even if imperfect; we are not without a system of law; and we still for the most part hope our children may go onward and upward. Our purpose, therefore, ought to be to continue upon that long and erratic path of improvement that began for us roughly with the Renaissance. To imagine that our course will find only fair winds and sunny horizons would be childish. There will be good and bad moments. That's life. Let's try to imagine what the good might be.

The *size* of government is an issue. If Milton Friedman's inquiry into the matter was about right, if we judge by the musings of the philosophers of the Enlightenment, and if we think the founders of the American republic still have something worthwhile to communicate to us, *government is now too large for any good it does us*. This implies trade-offs; nothing is free. The benchmark is the greater good of the greater number, and when we speak of an advantage we might derive from smaller government, we mean that for the majority there will be an advantage. Everyone will be able to point to someone who will suffer. That isn't the question. It is rather whether for each who suffers, there are not two whose lot improves. That, beyond providing some sort of safety net whereby food and shelter are available to the destitute, is about the best we can hope for. Societies are properly constituted for the greater good of the greater number. It is a fool's errand to think one can provide for the good of all. It cannot be done, and trying brings more harm than good.

If we grant this thesis, that the size of our modern governments is more a problem than a benefit, we must try to understand how to confront the issue, since no privilege once granted is ever easily relinquished. Our government will not just melt away sui generis. It will have to be melted away. There is only one thing for it. As in certain cancers, one must take away the blood supply upon which the tumor feeds. For government, this means money. In various ways, the capping of spending has been fitfully attempted over the last thirty years with only small success. The need is for a constitutional limit on spending. Imagine—and I am well aware that this is beyond the orbit of what is for now practicable—an amendment to the Constitution would prohibit the sum of all taxes and fees imposed by all levels of government to exceed, for example, twenty-five percent of national income. As I said, for now, for all the reasons we have discussed, this simply ain't happenin'. It might at some future time, perhaps when the people come to realize that there is no money left. Much water will pass beneath the bridge first.

There are steps we might take in the direction of smaller and more benign government. The reform of the tax system such that the one actually paying the bill sees the entire bill, in one clear amount, and writes a check for it, would surely constrain the spendthrift ways of government. Getting this done would not be easy. It would mean breaking the stranglehold professional politicians have on us.

To break the politicians' stranglehold, we must limit their time in office, and we must limit the advantage they personally draw from office. Term limits are not broadly applied, yet we have one for the highest office in the land. We would be well advised to have limits for all the offices in the land. This is within the realm of what might be possible. It would require a strong voice leading us to it. The notion of term limits has been applied throughout history—not nearly enough, it's true—with some success. The Ottomans governed reasonably well for some centuries with this notion.

The new factor is that of Western democracy. Do we wish to preserve the advantages it has brought? If yes, we must act to protect democratic institutions. Permanence in office is antithetical to such institutions. The professional politician has an instinctive lust for power, and that lust inevitably deprives us of our rights. There is only one thing for it: throw the bastard out!

Moreover, the holding of political office ought never to be the best job (i.e., best compensated) that a person might have. Serving in public office ought to imply some sacrifice. We have far too many politicians for whom their political office is the best job to which they could aspire. We pay too much, and we grant too many privileges. A suggestion would be that the wage of the politician ought to be that of the average American family. Would there not be justice in that? It also has the advantage of being self-adjusting—so none of that "voting themselves pay increases" nonsense. The better the American family does, the better our politicians can do.

We could say that the proposal immediately here above—that pay be aligned with that of the American family—would not suffice, given the costs of living away from home part of the year, to allow a poor man to serve in high office. Point taken. Thus, with regard to legislatures, let them be in session for no more than three months each year, preferably biennially. The important business can easily be taken care of in such time, and the limitation of time will sharply curtail the mischief they otherwise get up to. Such an arrangement would allow citizen-legislators to keep their day jobs, not incidentally keeping them in touch with our reality. Self-evidently, we would not be so tight as not to pay them a *modest* housing and travel allowance, for the very purpose of assuring that rich and poor can serve us equally.

Our system of justice, of law, needs reform. We drown in a sea of unnecessary procedure and venal litigation. Three changes could undo much of the damage.

First, in court, the loser pays. The trial lawyers will caterwaul about this one, confirming us in our opinion that it's the right thing to do. It's a notion that has long existed in the United Kingdom, whose body of law is extremely similar to our own, English common law. It's simple: if a man brings an action against another, let him be confident of his ground, for should he lose, he shall pay.

Second, let all civil litigation be heard before judges, not juries. No more tear jerking, no more circuses in front of the gallery. Trials would be shortened and simplified. The playacting of attorneys would be kept for criminal cases.

Third, let damages in civil cases not exceed actual damages. How to effect the reforms? It won't be easy. Remember that a majority of our legislators are attorneys. They will vote their profession's interest, not ours. Oh, to be sure, they'll concoct all sorts of reasons for protecting their pockets, but we mustn't be sensitive to their wailing. There's only one thing for it, and it won't be easy: the people must insist. A leader must be found to lead. A legislature of citizen-legislators would vote the reform in a heartbeat. Maybe we must begin with that.

A permit, as for a power plant, once legally granted, may not be further challenged nor revoked but for failure to comply with its conditions. This is really a corollary of sorts to the constitutional bar upon bills of attainder.

Spending measures must be fully funded.

Incarceration for victimless crime and crime that poses no physical threat to the public peace must be eliminated. It achieves no benefit for us and costs us grievously. (The matter of whether victimless crime ought to be crime at all deserves our entire consideration.)

We must address the issue of individual privacy. If we wish to remain free, a society constituted in liberty, we must find a way to incorporate the most adamantine safeguards for privacy into our Constitution. This is material for our Bill of Rights if ever there was any!

All public accounts should be corrected for inflation.

With these changes, we would renew our republic, restore our democracy, and ensure a very large step forward, for many generations, in the prosperity of the nation. Realistically, proceeding from today's base, it cannot be done. Truly, the world is stupid. In fact, there is only one way in which it might come to be done, following Jefferson's wise if wistful recommendation that the only way to ensure liberty is a revolution from time to time. We need a revolution. It does not need to be bloody, and in fact in a democracy it ought not to be, but it must be a revolution nonetheless.

Historically, only one thing will pave the way: a cup brimming with dissatisfaction. For the present, we can't see it. History, however, is full of examples of dissatisfaction, sometimes unexpected, that rather suddenly reared up and opened the door for change. Within recent memory, the United States had such an episode, the Carter years, which led to the Reagan years. The big issue, successfully resolved, was the Cold War. In 1979 it might have easily been thought that we had little choice but to become another Finland in our modus vivendi with the Soviet Union. In a single ballot, we changed that. A man led us with a different view.

Will the extreme government spending of today, here and abroad, lead to another yet more severe financial crisis than the present one? It does not have to be wished for to acknowledge that it may do so. And then? When there's no public money left? When nation-states are effectively bankrupt? Wouldn't that set the stage for a revolution?

One thing is certain: large government is inefficient. It may take China and India becoming the dominant economic powers of our world to teach it to us. We may react to the competition. Challenged, we would have to adopt the policies that ensure competitive success. In any case what is inefficient is ultimately replaced by the more efficient. It is a natural law. Success wins. Individual right underpins success: life, liberty, and the pursuit of happiness.

Postscript
What if I Am Wrong?

It is the indispensable question: What if I am wrong? Kipling had it right: "If you can trust yourself when all men doubt you, but make allowance for their doubting too ... then you'll be a man my son."

The purpose of my thoughts has been avowedly polemical. In no instance have I meant personal injury or insult to any man. I have addressed matters of public policy with impatience, irritation, and a measure of intemperance. What I would not do is to shout down any other for his opinion—something from which those I have roundly castigated might learn. Our public discourse must be vigorous and well fought. Within the list of reforms I included in the final chapter, I might—I was tempted—have added reforms to education. Our children are no longer taught to think. We imagine that a course in classical philosophy would be far beyond our high-school students, yet it was once common. History isn't what now entertains the PC crowd. It is what brought us here, the remarkable founding thought and documents of the nation.

The point is that a free people, to remain free, must be capable of rational argumentation and dialogue. We cannot deny the role emotion plays, but we can—as I have tried to suggest—see that grown-ups with a grown-up understanding be in charge. What is grown-up? The antithesis of childish, the understanding that one cannot have the cake and eat it too.

The place of economics in our public life cannot be underestimated. We have examined how liberty without property cannot be. Property is fundamentally economic. When we do not understand economics, when we do not know that economic laws are as real and inviolable as the physical laws of nature, we invite hardship. The tendency of social democracies to see money with a jaundiced eye must be *philosophically* countered. There is no evil in money. Money is man's labor in another form. We all have the notion of the integrity and justness of honorable labor. Why do we then pretend that its fruit is bitter?

The promise of technology cannot be overlooked. If we consider what we have wrought in the last one hundred years, who can doubt that the next hundred will be ever much more marvelous? The knowledge of humanity doubles every decade or so now. Do we expect imagination and creation to suddenly halt? It is absurd to make decisions now based on what we can imagine conditions will be in fifty, one hundred, or two hundred years. In fact, we have no idea. One of the greatest frustrations in any dialogue with pessimists—the prophets of doom—is that they inevitably suppose that the natural world and our place in it are static. They are everything but. If we must become frantic every time some butterfly is found a little beyond its natural range—if natural range can even be more than semantic—we shall need an evergreen Xanax prescription. The natural world is defined by change, not by stasis. It is difficult to comprehend that anyone can know so little of nature and nature's world not to see this.

There is no doubt that man has not always been kind to his planet. It is our common home, and we share a trust in which we mustn't fail. This said, prosperity seems to be the key: the more a nation is prosperous, the more it can tend to the challenges it faces. The poor suffer not only individually but collectively, too. Our best path—morally, economically, environmentally—will be to ensure the prosperity of the world's peoples. Anyone who has played on a beach as a child knows that building a castle is more satisfying than trying to scoop a hole in the sand.

It would be surprising indeed if everything I have affirmed is correct. I can only say that it is correct to the best of my knowledge and that my intention in declaring it has been one of good faith. I have had the privilege of traveling the world and observing its ways. I have seen what works and what doesn't work. I have seen prosperity and poverty. I have seen the oppression that causes poverty. I have contempt and a visceral hatred for dictators. Foolishness makes me irascible and intemperate. Yet I am forever an optimist—perhaps an optimistic fool through the writing of these thoughts—and a great believer in the triumph of man.

Claude Roessiger
December 22, 2009